People Speak 7

Titles in this series:

People Speak 7

Chaim Walder

Translated into English by Aviva Rappaport

People Speak 7/Chaim Walder

Originally published in Hebrew as Sipurim MeiHaChaim 7. Translated into English and Edited by Aviva Rappaport
First printed in Israel on 2014

ISBN 10: 1-50558-228-8
ISBN 13: 978-1505582284

Contact: Wold2015@gmail.com

Contents

1

Bride in Black on White

M y story goes back fifty years. At that time, it was the talk of the town here in Eretz Yisrael. Rumors swept the country, but no one knew the real story.

The rumors were about a cup of black Turkish coffee that spilled on a bride's wedding gown shortly before the ceremony. Nowadays, maybe this wouldn't be big news. Today the media is so full of news items that a story like this wouldn't get much coverage. But times were different then. Life moved at a slower pace. People barely knew what went on beyond the streets of their own neighborhood, so when something like this happened, the story traveled by word of mouth from one neighborhood, city, and even country, to the next.

A lot of people thought it was made up. You know, one of those urban fables that people like to share, such as, for instance, the one about the man who found himself in a Turkish hotel and discovered that he'd been knocked out and had a kidney removed.

People like to talk about their deepest fears, and you'll have to agree with me that for a bride, getting a coffee stain on her wedding gown minutes before the *chuppah* is a very big worry, and I don't think it's something that happens that often, either.

But the story is true. I know because I was one of the four women there in the room when it happened.

The backstory is even bigger than a bridal gown getting stained a minute before the *chuppah*.

❋ ❋ ❋

It started with the ordinary engagement of an ordinary bride to an ordinary groom. Right after the engagement, the bride's mother went to a seamstress to order the gown.

The seamstress was a widow who lived a hard life, but who was very good at what she did. The bride's mother did not live a hard life, but she wasn't considered the easiest person to get along with. She had many good qualities. She was a good, devoted mother, but very, let's say, determined.

She hovered over the seamstress offering a steady stream of comments and criticisms, then was dissatisfied with the first result and told the seamstress to redo it. Finally, after months of work, when the finished gown arrived, the mother decided she didn't like it and went to a different seamstress, who was considered the best and most expensive at that time.

The first seamstress was very hurt by having her work rejected. It wasn't only the hours, days, weeks, and months of labor she'd put into it. She knew that beauty is in the eye of the beholder. Yet every craftsman awaits a few kind words of praise for his work. Here, not only had she worked twice as hard, but now she was about to receive the final blow: the complete rejection of her sewing creation.

The bride herself didn't say a thing to her mother. She was a good girl, respectful of her parents, but now she felt torn. The anguish of the seamstress broke her heart, but honoring her mother didn't allow her to comment. Her heart was bursting to say that causing distress to a widow was not what she wanted as part of her wedding. She wanted to step under the *chuppah* with as many good deeds as possible to her credit, not the opposite.

As if all this wasn't bad enough, the mother decided that it was within her rights not to pay the seamstress for the dress.

For the seamstress, that was the last straw. Bitterly discouraged, she went to the mother's sister, the bride's aunt, who was a *rebbetzin*, and asked for her help.

The *rebbetzin* told her sister that she was making a very serious mistake. The emotional damage caused by rejecting the dress, as well as the financial damage of withholding wages, were grave wrongs.

The bride's mother didn't listen to her sister. She became angry at her, and told her that she didn't have to accept a garment that wasn't perfect. She asked her sister not to meddle in her affairs.

The bride witnessed the entire conversation and was deeply disturbed.

She knew that she was going to walk to her *chuppah* in a bridal gown that was not only sewn by a famous seamstress, but was incomparably more beautiful than the rejected one. Yet, sewn in with the stitches was a widow's shame. This made her sad and distressed, and, to tell you the truth, filled her with foreboding. She pictured evil angels hovering over the *chuppah* pointing accusing fingers, saying that her happiness included a mortal blow to the widow.

Gently, she tried to broach the subject with her mother, but her mother cut her off. "I don't want to hear another word about it. If you want to honor me, then don't bring up the subject again."

The bride, good girl that she was, said nothing more, but quietly ate her heart out. She ached for the widowed seamstress, and, at the same time, trembled with fear for herself. As the day of the wedding neared, instead of feeling like a happy bride, she was anxious and tormented.

Meanwhile, she dragged herself after her mother to the new seamstress for fittings. The more beautiful her new gown looked – and it was very beautiful – the worse she felt. *What will be?* she asked herself. *What good is a fancy gown whose price includes ugly conduct?* She had no answer.

The wedding day arrived. Two hours before the ceremony, the bride was at home making final preparations. Though she wore the snowy white bridal gown, her heart was blacker than black.

Around her fluttered her mother, her aunt, and a professional makeup artist, all busy making sure that the bride would truly look like a princess. Only she was tormented by thoughts of the widow sitting at home staring at the rejected bridal gown, the fruits of her labor.

It happened an hour before the wedding.

A cup of now-cold black coffee found its way from a nearby table onto the snowy white gown, leaving an ugly black stain.

Three of the four women screamed. Only one was rendered shocked into silence – the bride herself.

"I'm so sorry," the bride's aunt, the *rebbetzin*, said. "I didn't see it sitting there. I reached over to the bouquet of flowers, and I must have accidently knocked it over. I don't believe it."

The mother, after her exclamations of horror, stared in shock at the large coffee stain. She turned on her sister furiously. "Why weren't you more careful?" she hissed. "You've ruined the wedding."

"Ima," the bride protested, but said no more.

"What are we going to do now?" the mother wailed. "A bride without a gown is like a wedding without a groom."

The aunt, the *rebbetzin*, was the first to recover. "We have the first dress. I'll run over to the seamstress to get it. I hope she didn't give it to someone else."

She stood up and left, and ran to get the dress.

Three women were left in the room. Three women – and an elephant of suspicion that everyone knew was there. Everyone knew that the mother didn't believe her sister for one minute. It was no accident, of that she was sure. She hadn't forgotten how her sister had pressured her to take that first dress and to pay the seamstress. Her expression spoke louder than words. But suspicion was all it remained. After all, what proof did she have?

Twenty minutes passed before the aunt returned from the seamstress. No one had time to settle accounts right then. Their only concern was to exchange the coffee-stained gown for a glistening white one.

Within half an hour, the bride was ready to leave the house, slightly behind schedule and wearing a bridal gown much less fancy than the first. However, anyone looking at her closely would see a glowing bride filled with happiness. She looked every inch the radiant bride…and a bit more.

The wedding took place, and it was especially joyous. Everyone knew about the spilled coffee that had almost destroyed the bride's happiness and the miracle of so quickly finding a replacement gown. No one wondered exactly how they'd found a gown that hadn't needed any alterations yet fit so perfectly or how they'd known where to find it. In the eyes of the wedding guests, they'd witnessed a miracle, and the story of "the coffee that spilled right before the wedding" spread throughout the country – fifty years ago, that is – and it was the most exciting news of those days.

No one knew about the backstage drama that took place with the gown, the seamstress, the mother of the bride, the aunt, the bride herself, and, of course, the cup of coffee – the coffee that darkened the dress but lightened the wedding, at least as far as the bride was concerned.

❀　　❀　　❀

But the story doesn't end there. After the wedding and *sheva berachos*, the mother started keeping her distance from her sister, the *rebbetzin*. At first, their lack of contact appeared to be by chance. Gradually, it became obvious that the mother was mad at her sister and had decided not to have anything more to do with her.

Attempts were made at reconciliation, but they met with adamant refusal on the part of the bride's mother, and during one of the stronger attempts, the truth came out.

"I know that she did it on purpose," the mother said. "I'm absolutely certain of it. Only I know the pressure she put on me between the engagement and the wedding. In the beginning, she asked nicely. Then she began reprimanding me. In the end, she started lecturing me, and finally she spoke harshly to me. When I refused, she brutally forced me to use the other gown. I don't want to have anything to do with someone who dares spill a cup of coffee on a bride's gown minutes before the wedding. She's crazy. That's all there is to say about it. She couldn't control herself and has no self-restraint. I'm never going to talk to her again. She's not my sister anymore."

There was no real contact between them after that. The mother of the bride tried to force those around her to cut off contact with the aunt too, but it didn't work. Everyone told her, "We don't agree with what you're doing, and we won't be a party to it." The bride, more than anyone, developed a close relationship with her aunt, for reasons well understood. It was the only time someone had dared stand up to her mother's dominance and anger.

❈   ❈   ❈

The years passed, and children were born to the bride. The children grew up, married, and brought her grandchildren and great-grandchildren. The story of the coffee made its way through the family with a smile – though they all knew the smile ended at the doorstep of the matriarch of the family.

The now elderly mother of the bride lived with her daughter, the heroine of the story. The entire family devoted themselves to caring for her in as she grew steadily weaker.

And as she weakened, she softened, and her daughter felt that the time had come for a conversation that had waited decades.

"Ima," the daughter said, "do you remember my wedding day with the cup of coffee that spilled?"

"Of course I remember it," the mother said. "You never forget something like that."

"Do you remember how you blamed my aunt for spilling the coffee on purpose?"

"Yes," the mother said. "And don't try to tell me that the coffee spilled all by itself! Do me a favor. I may be old and sick, but I'm not stupid."

"That's okay, Ima," the daughter said. "I'm not going to tell you that the cup fell over by itself. It was done on purpose. I myself saw it happen. I can't deny it. You were right. The coffee was spilled deliberately."

"Finally! At long last someone testifies to the truth," the mother said with a sigh of relief. "I've been telling everyone for years that my sister spilled the coffee and that it wasn't an accident. No one could understand why I quarreled with her. I don't know what took you so long to admit this."

"I'll tell you why, Ima. The person who forbade me from telling the truth was your sister. That's the only reason I didn't tell you."

"You see? Now do you understand why I was so angry with her all these years? If only she'd have admitted it. Not only did she do what she did, but she made sure that my own daughter wouldn't tell me the truth. Do you see what type of person we're dealing with here?"

"Ima," the daughter said, "there's a different reason why she told me not to tell you what really happened. It's because the truth is that the coffee was deliberately spilled, but she didn't spill it."

"She didn't? *Then who did?*" the mother nearly shouted.

"I did."

"What?"

"I was so scared and sad. I didn't know how I was going to walk to the *chuppah* wearing a bridal gown soaked with a widow's tears. I honored you, Ima. I tried to tell you, but you didn't want to hear it. I had no other way to prevent it, so I just spilled the coffee on the gown. It was me, Ima, not her."

"Then...then why are you telling me this only now?"

"Because my aunt's sharp eyes caught what I had done and she put a finger to her lips signaling me to keep silent. When she found a quiet moment, she whispered to me, 'I saw it. Don't say a word. It could destroy the wedding for both you and your mother.' A few months after the wedding, I tried to convince her to let me tell you the truth, but she made me promise not to. 'If she's mad at me because she only suspects me of spilling the coffee, she'll be *very* upset with you if she finds out you did it deliberately. For her sake and yours, it's best that you have a good relationship.'

"Over the years, I've asked her at various times if she'd agree to let me tell you, but she's never said yes. Only recently, when I told her that I must tell you the truth and that now you're less likely to get upset, did she agree."

The great-grandmother and her sister made up that very same day. The great-grandmother cried over her years of stubbornness that had denied her a relationship with her sister. At the same time, she admitted that the alternative – quarreling with her daughter – would have been worse.

A few months later, she passed on, but not before asking that this story be told so that people would learn how important it is to be flexible and not rigid.

A year later, her sister passed on. Two out of the three who knew the real story are no longer alive.

I'm the only one left to tell the story, and if you haven't figured out who I am by now, I'll tell you.

I was the bride.

2

The Farmer

My story takes place eleven years ago. My brother was then a nineteen-year-old *yeshivah bachur,* considered one of the best boys in his yeshivah. He learned straight through, from dawn till dusk, and well into the night too. He didn't sleep much at all, but that didn't stop him from getting up on time for davening and putting in a full day.

We were all very proud of him. He'd always been a studious, well-behaved kid, only interested in learning and growing spiritually. In *yeshivah ketanah,* he was the *ilui* of the yeshivah, and in *yeshivah gedolah,* he only got better. He learned nonstop, davened with deep concentration, and never wasted time or got sidetracked by other interests.

When the *mashgiach* called my father, it came as a surprise. He said he wanted to bring to my father's attention his concern that my brother might have a problem.

My father traveled to the yeshivah, where the *mashgiach* told him that my brother's intense focus and time spent learning were worrisome. Strong learning is good, he said, but exaggeration in any area isn't. He said that my brother hardly ate, to the point where it was endangering his health. He slept very little, and wasn't part of the *chevra*.

"Based on my experience," he told my father, "we shouldn't let the piety and strong learning blind us, but should make sure that he isn't endangering his physical and mental health."

My father talked with my brother, but it was like talking to a wall. All of a sudden, my brother, the epitome of good *middos* and *derech eretz*, opened his mouth to my father like he'd never done before. He dismissed all those whose job it was to guide him and mold him and explained where they were wrong and why he hadn't reached even half of what Hashem expected from him. He went on and on lecturing my father, who by now was very worried.

When my father said he agreed with the *mashgiach*, my brother turned his sharply worded criticism at him and began to lecture him in a *chutzpadik* way, saying things my father never dreamed he'd hear from a son, and certainly not this one. My father left there numb with shock, but one thing was clear: If he didn't take action, my brother was headed for a nervous breakdown.

Now began a long, tiring journey that included consultations with well-known rabbinical figures, most of whom were "disqualified" by my brother, who irrationally saw them as people whose goal was to weaken his learning. Some, whom he could in no way disqualify, he claimed had been prejudiced against him by whatever my parents must have told them, and therefore he had no obligation to listen to them.

My brother's mental health deteriorated. He hardly ate, and became a skeletal figure with dark circles under his eyes and a haunted look. Finally, in consultation with my parents, the yeshivah told him that he could no longer continue there unless he got treatment.

He came home angry at the world and locked himself in his room, leaving only for davening. He didn't come out to eat, not even on Shabbos. My mother left his meals outside his door, but he barely touched them. The psychiatrists my parents consulted advised them to commit him to a closed psychiatric ward against his will.

My father was determined to do everything possible to avoid reaching that point. With guidance from a professional specializing in behavioral disorders, they began a program that included removing the door to my brother's room and actually forcing him – not always gently – to leave the house for a few hours a day.

He struggled, he fought, and he raged against my parents, who suffered in silence and did not respond. They did only what they were instructed to do.

Then, one day, he disappeared.

That day is one I'll never forget. At first, my parents weren't concerned. They thought he was testing them, trying to scare them. But when he didn't call or come home that night, they contacted the police.

A few nerve-wracking days later, during which we had no idea where he was, the police decided to declare him a missing person. They contacted the media with an appeal for information, and soon his picture and personal information were everywhere.

Yes, it was embarrassing, but we were willing to do anything we could to find him.

My parents' suffering was painful to see. They spent every waking minute looking for him, and barely ate or slept.

But my brother had disappeared as if the ground had swallowed him up.

❄   ❄   ❄

Now I want to fill you in on what was happening to my brother at this time. He'd left the house without any money, wearing a suit and hat and carrying his tefillin bag. He started to walk on a major highway without knowing where it led to or how fast the cars were going. He walked and walked for a few hours until a driver pulled over next to him and asked him where he wanted to go.

"To the end of the road," my brother said.

The driver took him to the end of the road and let him off. My brother started walking across the fields that bordered the road. It's not clear how long he walked, but according to what we pieced together later, he must have walked for about eight hours straight (!) from when the driver let him off. He kept on going, growing weaker, until he collapsed, and lay there unconscious.

Later, the police told us that the chances of his remaining alive on that kind of a hike without food or water were zero.

He woke up in a nice big bed in a spacious room, and the first thing that met his eyes were two farmers who looked like father and son, one fat and the other skinny.

The skinny one gave him a glass of water. "Here, drink. Drink something. You drank a lot already, but I think you're still dehydrated."

"Where am I?" he asked.

"You're in a safe place," the older man told him. "One of the workers found you twelve hours ago. You had passed out a few yards from the fence. He brought you here. We woke you up and gave you water to drink, and then we laid you down here in this bed to sleep. It's a miracle they didn't shoot you."

"Shoot me? Why should they shoot me?"

"Don't you know why?" the farmer asked him.

"No."

"Don't you recognize me?"

"No. Why should I? Have I ever met you?"

The farmer and his son laughed. "Okay," the farmer said, "let's get some food into you."

A maid brought in a plate of food, a hot dog omelet. My brother shrank back and said, "I can't eat here. I don't know what the *hechsher* is."

"Oh, yeah. Right," the skinny one said. "Can you eat Angel's bread?"

"Yes."

"How about Tnuva cheese?"

"Let me see the container."

They started bringing containers and packages of food into the room for my brother to check. For every one he approved, three were rejected. In the end, he had the makings of a meal. Naturally, he asked for paper plates and plastic cutlery. Then he washed his hands and dug in.

When he had eaten his fill, they asked him if he wanted to call home.

My brother said no.

They asked him why.

He said he'd run away from his parents.

"I see that you're *chareidi*," the farmer said. "Your parents probably forced you to pray and learn all day, huh?"

My brother was confused. "Uh, not exactly," he said. "In fact, they did the exact opposite."

"The opposite?"

"Yes, the opposite. They think I'm learning and praying too much. They're fighting with me and trying to bring me down spiritually."

The farmer and his son now knew with whom they were dealing. They told my brother he had to talk to his parents.

He dug in his heels, and they didn't push him. Being in a somewhat isolated place, they didn't know people were searching for him, especially since the search didn't make the headlines but only appeared in small ads on the back pages of the newspapers.

The next day, my brother felt well enough to put on tefillin, daven, and walk outside. He saw that the farmer owned a vast tract of land with thousands of head of sheep and cattle, orchards, and fields of cotton.

That afternoon, the farmer appeared again and asked him if he'd like a guided tour of the place. The fat farmer drove him around in an ATV, proudly showing him his big farm. Along the way, they encountered a solitary grave.

"My wife is buried here," the farmer said.

"They let you bury her here in the yard?"

The farmer laughed. "I wouldn't exactly call it a yard. As you can see, I've got close to a thousand acres here, which is more than half the size of the city you live in."

"How did you get permission?"

"I didn't *get* permission, I *gave* permission."

On the way back, the farmer said to him, "Today you'll call your parents. I'm sure they're very worried about you. You'll need to tell me who they are and give me your home phone number. I'm sure they're good parents who want only what's best for you."

My brother agreed.

They went back to the house. My brother gave him the phone number, and the farmer called our home.

Now I'll pick up our side of the story from where I left off.

After two and a half days of not knowing where my brother was, we were very worried and feared the worst. All this time, the police had refused to conduct a search. Plenty of boys his age, they said, run away, only to return in a few days. But now they prepared to search.

Suddenly, the phone rang. My mother picked up.

"Shalom. Am I speaking with the lady of the house?"

The voice was unfamiliar, yet at the same time very familiar. My mother couldn't place it, though.

"Yes," she said.

"This is Ariel Sharon." Ariel Sharon was then prime minister of Israel.

"Gabi, this is no time for fooling around," my mother said. Gabi is a cousin who knows how to impersonate famous people, and Sharon was one of his favorites. My mother was sure this was another one of his pranks.

"Ha, ha, ha," the man laughed, just like the real thing. "Listen, I'm not Gabi, and I'm not imitating him. I'm really Ariel Sharon, and your son is here with me at the farm. I'm handing him the phone so you can talk to him."

My mother nearly fainted, but she still didn't believe it. All her misgivings vanished at the sound of my brother's voice saying, "Ima, I'm here. Everything's okay."

My mother burst into tears. "What are you doing at his house? How did you get to him?"

"To who?"

"To the prime minister."

"Ima, I'm here with a farmer. I'm in the south. I traveled south, and then I walked until I passed out."

"I want you to come home. We're so worried about you."

They talked for a few minutes, and then my brother handed the phone back to Ariel Sharon.

"Don't worry, lady," the familiar voice said. "We took good care of him, and we'll see that he gets back home safely. I think you need to get him treated."

"We're trying," my mother said. "We've been trying for a few years. He refuses all treatment. Maybe if you, as prime minister, order him to get treatment he'll listen."

He laughed his famous laugh and said, "But he doesn't even know I'm the prime minister. At first I thought he was pulling my leg, but then I saw he really had no idea who I am. How did you manage to raise a child here in Israel who doesn't know who the prime minister is?"

"I'm sorry," my mother said, "but we don't have a radio and we try not to bring newspapers into the home. I have two children who actually do know, but as for the rest… Well, they're all busy learning and aren't really interested in things like that. I'll try to tell them, though."

He laughed long and hard. "Don't you dare," he said finally. "What I like most is that there are places connected to other things entirely. Ask your rabbis. I always tell them that if there weren't yeshivos, the Jewish people would cease to exist. I'm not making this up, you know. I say it repeatedly. I also support army exemption for yeshivah students."

Sharon gave my mother the number of his personal aide and said that her son would return home the following day.

That night, Sharon talked with my brother. He wanted to understand how it was possible for him not to recognize him and to have no idea who the prime minister was. He found it amusing. At first, my brother thought he was putting him on, but then Sharon's son brought a newspaper and showed him a picture of the fat farmer, this time wearing fancy clothes. The caption read, "The prime minister leaving the weekly cabinet meeting." That got my brother to believe him.

Sharon told him to listen to his parents, because they had his best interests at heart. He also said that while personally he didn't have the good fortune to be religious or do mitzvos, he had a warm relationship with rabbis and Torah scholars, and he knew they were essential to the survival of the Jewish people.

The next morning, Sharon came into the room to say good-bye. My brother was in the middle of putting on tefillin. The prime minister waited patiently and then took him out to his limousine. They drove to the center of the country escorted by a long motorcade. My brother's head was spinning from the experience. On the way, my brother got out of the prime minister's car and entered a different car that took him home.

❋   ❋   ❋

This experience marked the beginning of a change in my brother. He agreed to go for treatment, and within a few months, he was able to return to yeshivah. He remained the same pious, dedicated learner, but thanks to the treatment, he knew that in his case, *bitulo zehu kiyumo* (what seems to be a diminishing of Torah actually represents an increase in Torah). Lowering his impossible standards of perfection would enable him to learn more Torah and do more mitzvos in the long run. He learned to set appropriate limits for himself and find a balance. Once again, he began to thrive in yeshivah, still a *masmid*, but now a friendly, personable guy who fit in.

Today, my brother is happily married, has several children, and learns in one of the best *kollels*.

The point here is not to judge the man Sharon and his complex life, but just to tell one small story about the Jewish spark that exists in each and every Jew, and the great merit that can come about from a caring talk. That's why, after Sharon passed away, my brother gave me permission to tell you his amazing story about those few days he spent at Sycamore Ranch – which for him became the "Sick No More" Ranch.

3

Treasures of the Kosel

As you already know, Mr. Walder, my wife and I go to the Kosel every single day – only when we feel up to it, that is, and aren't suffering from any of the aches and pains common to folks our age.

For years we walked, but lately we've been getting there by car. Don't think for a minute that we're taking taxis. No, people kindly offer to take us there. In fact, ever since you started putting our stories in your books, we have our pick of drivers, so at least one good thing came from all that scribbling.

In recent months, my wife has been complaining about how hard it is for her to reach her regular spot in the women's section on Rosh Chodesh. She's used to making her way slowly along the big stones for the purpose of... Well, you already know which purpose. I don't need to remind you each time about the notes she pulls out from the cracks and reads so that she can help whoever wrote them. But this doesn't negate the fact that she has a regular place, and as she walks, someone makes sure she gets to it.

But lately, because a few eccentric women want to insult the Kosel every Rosh Chodesh, a situation has developed where thousands of girls arrive early in the morning, making the place even more crowded than it is on Shavuos. The goal is a holy one, and my wife and I fully support it. Yet that doesn't change the fact that my wife has a hard time squeezing through the crowd to get to her place.

Despite the difficulty, though, she always manages to get right up to the Kosel. How, you're asking? I'll tell you. When the police see my wife coming – which takes them all of ten to twelve seconds – they order their men to clear a path for her.

I'm sure you're wondering, *Why would the security forces give his wife the VIP treatment?* Soon you'll come to all sorts of conclusions that we have something to do with Zionism.

That's why I want to tell you the whole story. Once you hear it, you'll know why my wife gets special treatment from the security forces.

❋   ❋   ❋

It all started with old Blumenfeld, may he rest in peace, owner of a moving company. Blumenfeld used to search the cracks of the Kosel every day for – no, not what you're thinking. Not notes. Those belong to my wife, and Blumenfeld never would have dreamed of encroaching on her territory. Why? For two reasons: One, Blumenfeld lived in Meah Shearim, and just as he wouldn't want my wife to start a moving company, he wouldn't compete with her business; and two, Blumenfeld wouldn't spend even one thin dime on those notes that people push into the cracks. He's like most of Yerushalayim's residents, especially those of Meah Shearim, who view the strange custom of stuffing notes into the Kosel as an unbelievable waste of time as well as a prayer in vain. As far as I'm concerned, the only good reason to do it is for my wife. But how many notes can she read and how many people can she help? Maybe a thousandth of what is there.

By the way, my wife says that since you started publishing our stories, *more* notes are being put between the Kosel stones. I think the opposite is true, but don't tell my wife, for obvious reasons.

But let me tell you why Blumenfeld searched the stones every single day. He was looking for money. Yes, money that people stuffed into the cracks.

This closely guarded secret is known only to a select few: the residents of Meah Shearim and its immediate vicinity.

Blumenfeld made his discovery when the Kosel first became accessible in 1967. (Before that, no one had money for seltzer water, let alone to push between rocks.) Blumenfeld happened to find a few lirot between the stones, and ever since, rumor has it that he's taken out millions. Others claim that Blumenfeld found money between the stones once or twice in 1967, but that in all the years he's trudged there every morning since, he hasn't found a single lira more. Despite that, he keeps it up, because someone who's won the lottery once can't stop buying tickets.

Blumenfeld, who, as I told you, was the owner of a well-known moving company, had a regular driver who used to take him to make his daily rounds of the Kosel stones. He kept this up from the day the Kosel was opened until the day he died – Blumenfeld, not the driver.

Don't think he needed the money. He had money like sand. After all, he was Blumenfeld of the moving company, wasn't he? Even if what they say is true, that a Yerushalmi doesn't forgo the opportunity to make a little money even if he's as rich as Korach, I still think he did it only for the *geshmak* of it.

Anyway, one day Blumenfeld complained to me that a few people wanted to take over the stones at the Kosel. I was shocked, and told him to call the police immediately, maybe even the army if he'd discovered a terrible plot like that. Then I calmed down and said to him that if he wanted my opinion, I didn't think there was a chance of moving even one of the stones.

"Fool!" Blumenfeld said to me. "I'm not talking about the stones themselves. I'm talking about the money that's hiding between them. That money belongs to me, and those people have taken over my territory. They get there an hour earlier and get to it first. That's why I haven't found anything lately."

I found myself wondering how much Blumenfeld had paid for the rights to collect money from between the Kosel's stones. I pushed away such thoughts with a firm hand and refrained from commenting. I only suggested to him that he report the theft to the police.

"It's not that simple," Blumenfeld said. "First of all, I know this government, and I don't think they'll help me. Second of all, if I go to the police, they may very well put some of their fancy jewelry on me, namely, handcuffs, and drag me with them to the Russian Compound. Look, I don't think that taking money from the Kosel stones is covered by law. They might try to ruin my reputation with all kinds of trumped-up charges. My hands are tied. I have no way to combat those thieves who've decided to get there before me."

Despite his convincing argument, my own personal feeling was that Blumenfeld was a bit off the mark in his accusations. I proceeded with the utmost caution and gently asked him if it might be better to call the people who were trying to find money between the stones "competitors."

Blumenfeld shot me a look of astonishment. "That's like telling Berel Cheshin to let other people take his buildings."

That statement shook me to the core. If someone were to tell me that my wife had found a bar of gold between the stones of the Kosel I'd be less surprised than by what Blumenfeld had just said about Berel Cheshin.

For your information, Berel Cheshin is one of Meah Shearim's most ragged schnorrers. He goes around with patched clothes and torn shoes. His beard is stained yellow from constant smoking, and only the smell of snuff competes with the fragrance of nicotine he exudes. If you had told me that he owned an old storage shed, I would have raised an eyebrow. But whole buildings?

"Really?" I said to Blumenfeld. "Berel Cheshin owns buildings?"

"Come on. Don't tell me you don't remember that Mottel the *shadchan* took him to *beis din*?"

Actually, I did remember something. But Mottel the *shadchan* spent all day in *beis din* suing people for not paying his *shadchan gelt*. Why? Because Mottel felt that if the idea to suggest one person to another crossed his mind, then he already deserved to be paid under the law that a good thought is worth its weight in gold. Also, plenty of people find all sorts of crazy excuses to avoid paying the *shadchan gelt*.

"So," Blumenfeld continued, "as you know, Berel Cheshin had a very hard time with *shidduchim* for his daughter. He promised Mottel that he'd give him a whole building if he managed to get her married. As you and I both know, if you offer Mottel double the price, he's liable to bring you the British crown prince himself after a kosher conversion – and even spruce up his reputation, which is harder than the conversion. So just imagine what he'll do for a whole building! That's why it wasn't long before Mottel brought Berel an excellent *bachur*, a real *masmid*, for his daughter. Who knows what kind of stories he had to think up for this one?

"After the *shidduch* was finalized, Mottel went joyfully to Berel and said, 'You remember what you promised me, don't you?'

And Berel said to him, 'Of course I remember. Come with me right now.' Mottel followed Berel expectantly until they reached Rechov Amos 6, at which point Berel said, 'This is the building I'm giving you. From now on, I won't collect at this spot. It's all yours.'"

After I laughed at Blumenfeld's joke, I understood which buildings Berel Cheshin "owned." And then, of course, I understood what Blumenfeld was getting at when he told me that the money between the stones of the Kosel belonged to him – just like Berel Cheshin's buildings belonged to *him*.

At that moment, I realized that the way to handle Blumenfeld's problem wasn't through legal channels but diplomatic ones, so I got Blumenfeld to give me the names of the people he was mad at, the ones he accused of stealing. They were a few fellows past their prime, real schlimazels with nothing better to do, who had reached the conclusion that Blumenfeld started his moving company from money he found between the stones of the Kosel. The way they talked, they'd gotten the raw end of the deal. You could hear their frustration at not finding even a single lira – which strengthens the opinion of the skeptics I mentioned at the beginning of the story.

I suggested, as a way of keeping the peace, that one way or another they find a different source of income, because what they were doing was causing anguish to Blumenfeld.

They asked for a few minutes to talk it over, and then they told me, "Okay. We agree, but on one condition."

"What's the condition?"

"Do you see Rabbi Getz sitting over there in the tunnel? Not a single person goes over to him to talk in *limud*. You're an important person, and we think that if you go over to him and spend half an hour learning with him, it will give him a very good feeling."

Mr. Walder, maybe you don't know who Rabbi Getz is. Rabbi Meir Yehuda Getz was the official rabbi of the Kosel from the minute we gained access to it in 1967. I was very close to him, in part to distract him from paying too much attention to the notes my wife takes such an interest in.

Naturally, I agreed to this condition. I was filled with admiration for these fellows who cared so much about the respect due the elderly rabbi. And to make it a condition for ending a business competition was truly commendable.

Anyway, I went over to Rabbi Getz, who was sitting there deep inside the tunnel, and started to talk Torah with him. He was quite a fine scholar. We went back and forth, with me checking my watch every so often to see if I had fulfilled my part of the bargain.

After twenty-five minutes, Rabbi Getz said to me, "You can stop now. They finished."

"They finished what?" I asked.

Rabbi Getz looked at me and smiled. "Don't you know why they sent you to me?"

I'd never felt so embarrassed in my life. *How does he know?* I asked myself.

Then he surprised me even more. "That bunch comes here every so often. They climb down ropes into the giant holes here and gather the coins that tourists throw in. Their only problem is that I sit here learning all the time. That's why they look for someone to keep me busy, whether by talking in learning or getting a nudnik to ask me silly questions. I may be old, but I'm not blind or deaf. Yet it suits me to have them think I don't know what they're up to."

"Are you trying to tell me that they played me for a fool?" I whispered to him.

"What did they sell you, that I'm lonely and looking for company?"

"Something like that," I admitted, red faced.

"*Nu*, I really enjoyed our time together, and they did too. The main thing is that they think I don't know what they're up to," Rabbi Getz said.

We burst out laughing, two old-timers sharing a private joke the youngsters could never understand.

"So why don't you do something about it?" I asked him.

"Why should it bother me if Jews are enjoying themselves? Does the Kosel belong to me? To my grandfather? What business is it of mine if someone looks for money here that doesn't belong to anyone, or if a woman wants to read notes? They're all good Jews – let them enjoy."

That was Rabbi Getz's way of telling me he knew all about my wife's routine. And here I'd thought I could outsmart him.

In a certain way, I was relieved that he knew. Before, I'd been afraid he'd find out. That's why I kept up such a good relationship with him. Now that I wasn't afraid anymore, our relationship became even better.

❈   ❈   ❈

You're probably wondering how all this is connected to the fact that the security forces at the Kosel take good care of me and my wife, aren't you?

We're getting to that.

Until a few years ago, the holes in the floor of the Kosel tunnels weren't covered with thick glass but with iron bars, which meant that people could throw money into them and also slide down into them on ropes. One day, I saw dozens of policemen standing around helplessly. One of the commanders of the police force had been standing there when a medal he'd earned in the line of duty fell into a pit. He was embarrassed. He didn't want to make use of the police force for his own personal needs, but on the other hand, to leave the premises without that hard-earned medal was unthinkable.

I went over to them, offered them some snuff, and then, *very gently* probed as to whether the medal was made of gold or diamonds for him to be worrying about it so much.

For some reason, my question amused them. They began coughing (from the snuff) and laughing (I have no idea why). He explained to me that this particular medal had sentimental value and was worth more to him than gold.

If you ask me, I wouldn't have wasted a penny on it, but, understandably, I didn't share this sentiment with the policemen, especially not with the worried-looking commander.

"Excuse me, sir," I said, "but I can solve your problem on condition that you don't ask any questions."

He readily agreed. "I'll move away from here with my men, and you do what has to be done. Anything to get back my medal. Of course, what I just said must remain between us."

I went to the pay phone and called one of the fellows who went down into the pits. I explained the situation to him and told him that if he accomplished the mission successfully, I'd talk to Rabbi Getz every time they wanted to go down into the pits. He didn't have to know that Rabbi Getz already knew what was going on.

He showed up less than ten minutes later with his friends and their ropes. They went down to the bottom of the pit, but they didn't come back up for a while. When the commander asked me what was taking them so long, I explained to him that as long as they were down there, they were doing their civic duty by cleaning the pit, picking up all kinds of papers and particularly *metal* items that had fallen there. The commander caught my meaning and started to laugh.

They came up twenty minutes later and gave the commander his medal. It was the first time a police commander was awarded a medal by a bunch of schlimazels. On second thought, maybe it wasn't the first time....

Since a lot of policemen were there, and they realized exactly how I'd helped their commander, I became friends with all of them. I passed around my snuff box again, we sneezed together, and ever since, they've given me the royal treatment. Whenever they get a new police chief for the Kosel, someone tells him, "This man and his wife get special treatment."

None of the young policemen was there at the rescue of the medal, but they know they have to give us special treatment, and that's good enough for me.

By the way, if anyone thinks he can go down into those pits to collect the money there, he'd better give up the idea fast. It would take an expert glassmaker or a thug with a sledge-hammer to break the glass, and the noise certainly wouldn't be of much benefit to Rabbi Getz's learning. Then again, Rabbi Getz hasn't been with us for many years.

On second thought, even if the glass were broken, they wouldn't find a single coin down there, because no one goes to the trouble of breaking glass to throw down money. Now why didn't you think of that?

In conclusion, tell your readers who come to the Kosel on Rosh Chodesh to protect it from those who want to offend it, and not to get mad if they see policemen clearing a path to the front row for a woman who is not all that young. It's just my wife trying to get to her usual spot, right next to the stones of the Kosel.

4

Broken Words, Broken Hearts

I'm thirty-five and currently hold a position in *chinuch*.

I've kept my story a deep, dark secret for most of my life and only recently decided to share it, because I'm certain that what I have to say will be of benefit to many people.

My parents didn't start off religious, but by the time I was born, they were. They raised me well, with lots of warmth and love.

When I was six years old, I was on a bus with my father when suddenly a man wearing a scary mask got on. He sat down right opposite us.

I was scared stiff. Actually, I was scared speechless. My father had no idea anything was wrong. At the time, I felt like I sat there for an eternity, frozen in my seat, unable to express how afraid I was. When we got off the bus, my father said to me, "What's going on?"

I didn't answer him.

It took a few minutes for him to realize that this wasn't the usual kid thing of not answering a question right away. He tried to get me to tell him what was happening, but I'd lost my ability to speak.

It took a few weeks before I could utter a peep, and when I did, my parents discovered that their son could talk, but with a severe stutter.

They thought it would pass, but they were wrong. I continued to suffer from a heavy stutter throughout my childhood. I couldn't get a single sentence out of my mouth without tripping over it. Talking in a group was out of the question, and when I reached bar mitzvah, everyone knew there was no chance of me *leining* the parasha or leading the davening.

I avoided talking, even with friends, because it created an uncomfortable situation. People who don't stutter probably can't understand what I'm talking about, because they've never been through it.

Usually, my classmates didn't try to mimic me or hurt my feelings, but if ever it did happen, my teachers quickly put a stop to it.

Eventually, my mother took me to a speech therapist, a very special woman named Tamar Berger, who was renowned in the field. Every week, my mother and I would go to see her, and the treatment started to help. I felt that I was making progress, albeit slow, in overcoming the stutter.

The speech therapist had all kinds of creative ways for getting around the stutter, such as slightly stretching the beginning sound of a word instead of getting stuck on it, using a different word that is easier to say, and inserting "bridge" words like *yes* and *so*.

I graduated elementary school and entered *yeshivah ketanah*.

That's when I encountered a problem that threw me way back to first base and almost ended the game.

It was a kid by the name of "Meir." Obviously, I'm not going to use his real name. In the very first week of yeshivah he caught on to my speech impediment and started to mimic me.

I'd been through stuff like that before, but unlike previous times, where it had stopped almost as soon as it started without much effort on my part, this didn't pass. Whether I reacted or not, he was there to make sure to embarrass me in public, to shed my blood, to imitate me, and to turn my stutter into something funnier, more entertaining, and weirder than it was.

He'd mimic the way I said my family name, which I always stumbled over. He'd stand at the entrance to the dining room and shout out at a volume that couldn't be missed, "Moshe Co-co-co-co-hen." (I'm making up this name too, and purposely using a common name.)

The only thing I could think of was to mimic him back, but, as you surely realize, that just proved that he'd succeeded in getting me upset, and made his attacks more frequent.

After one of the sessions, the speech therapist told my mother that the abusive treatment given me by my so-called friend was ruining any positive effects the sessions had and was making the stutter worse.

I once overheard her say to my mother that if I couldn't overcome the stutter now, it might stay with me my whole life. I felt like I was facing a cruel enemy that gave me no respite. You can't imagine to what extent I hated him.

He had supersensitive antennae that told him when I was going to a session, so that afterward he could come down on me even harder. In the dining room, at the entrance to the building, in every place possible, he would shout from one end of the room to the other, "Moshe Co-co-co-co-hen," and my heart would shatter into a thousand pieces time and time again.

❋　　❋　　❋

The speech therapist told my mother that if she wanted the treatment to be effective, I had to stay home for two days following every session. Otherwise, that boy would destroy everything I'd gained and make the problem worse.

The *mashgiach*, of course, noticed my three-day absence each week and asked my parents the reason. That's when he realized how serious the situation was.

I'd like to point out that over the years, the staff did try its best to stop the abusive behavior, but their warnings and punishments had no effect on Meir. His social standing was way up there because everyone was afraid of his big mouth and its power to put people down. He'd gotten it into his head to grind me into the ground, and nothing would stop him.

When I entered *shiur gimmel*, the speech therapist told my mother that I had to start leading the davening.

You can imagine how that went over with me. "I can't do it," I told my mother. "I'm living on another planet. How can I be the chazzan if I trip over every line?"

"I suggest we all go to the Kosel," the speech therapist said to my mother. "No one knows him there. I'll be able to hear where it's hard for him, and help him with it later."

We did as she said. The three of us made up to meet at the Kosel, where it's easy to form a minyan. I started to daven at the *amud*, standing fairly close to the women's section so the speech therapist could hear me from her side of the divider. She wrote down every place I got stuck.

And I got stuck a lot. By the time I finished, I was dripping with sweat. I felt like my heart would burst with suffering, and I found myself roaring, "Please, Hashem, let *him* feel what I'm going through!"

Now I know that despite the pain and suffering Meir caused me, I shouldn't have uttered such a prayer. But then, in my difficult situation, everything was too much for me, and I couldn't control myself.

Everyone – my parents, the other people at the Wall – was shocked. But no one said a thing.

✽   ✽   ✽

We left in silence. I realized I had reached my limit. Things couldn't go on like that anymore. I refused to discuss it with my parents.

That night, I tossed and turned, but by morning, I'd made my decision. I went to the *mashgiach* and told him, "HaRav, I know I haven't been putting my full efforts into learning, but I want to change. I'll make a deal with you. When the time comes, you find me a good yeshivah. I'm willing to sign an agreement with you that I'll make a total change."

We signed a contract. Just like that. With clauses and subclauses. I took myself in hand and changed.

The *mashgiach* was my *chavrusa* in the morning, and I had two other *chavrusos* for the second and third *sedarim*. I sat and learned without taking a break.

At the same time, I continued to work on my davening with the goal of becoming a chazzan. For instance, I would get stuck on the word *"ve'imru amen."* I learned to extend the *"i-i-i-i"* sound with a special melody that hid the stutter and to act as if it were part of the *nusach*. This took off some of the pressure on me.

Naturally, Meir was there to catch it. "Co-co-co-co-hen" became *"i-i-i-imru amen."* I've never encountered a kid so cleverly evil, but by then I didn't react.

The *mashgiach* would say to me, "Forget about him. He who laughs last, laughs best. Hold your head up. Don't look back. You'll make it. I guarantee it."

His constant encouragement motivated me to succeed.

✽   ✽   ✽

I finished three years of *yeshivah ketanah*. I was the only one in my *shiur* to be accepted by the best yeshivah, while Meir, along with another friend, was accepted by a less prestigious yeshivah.

As soon as I entered yeshivah, I formed a relationship with the *rosh yeshivah*, who drew me close with great warmth and friendship.

Exactly two days after the start of the *zman*, a friend from *yeshivah ketanah*, the one who'd gone with Meir to a different yeshivah, called me up.

"You're not going to believe what happened," he said.

"What happened?"

"Meir started to stutter."

I clicked off. Obviously Meir had gotten another friend to laugh at me.

He called me right back. "It's not a trick," he said. "He's really stuttering."

The truth is, even if I slightly believed him, I was fed up with the whole subject. "Whatever," I said. "I'm not interested in hearing about it." I clicked off again.

I went back into the *beis midrash* determined to continue as I'd done in *shiur gimmel*. The last thing I wanted to do was to think about Meir or anything connected with my past.

When I entered *yeshivah gedolah*, I felt a new surge of strength, both spiritually and in my learning, and, you'd be surprised to know, socially as well. In the *shiur* above mine, two *bachurim* had stutters much worse than mine. I started teaching them how to slowly stretch out a word like *loud*, how to almost sing a word, and how to stop and take a breath. I became their speech therapist, and I was pretty proud of it.

Two weeks after I arrived, I was told, "There's a *rosh yeshivah* here looking for you."

It was the *rosh yeshivah* of the yeshivah where Meir, the boy who had tormented me, learned. He had come to meet with me, and I knew what he wanted.

I fled the yeshivah and raced home, but not before sending a friend to tell the *rosh yeshivah* why I'd run away.

"I don't want to return to the past," I told my father, "and they're trying to force me to go there."

As I was talking, my *rosh yeshivah* called and said, "Please come to see me in the office."

❁   ❁   ❁

I went with my father. We arrived at the office and saw the two *roshei yeshivah* sitting there.

"Do you know what happened?" they said. "Meir's been stricken with a heavy stutter. He can hardly get a word out of his mouth. We're asking you to forgive him."

I started to cry. Everything exploded inside me. "My parents paid a fortune for my treatment! He murdered me! Did a delegation go to *him* to ask *him* to stop? What do you want from me?"

They were stunned by my outburst. My father asked me to leave, and he stayed with them. Half an hour later, they came out and said, "We apologize. We didn't know what you went through. We have no complaints against you if you don't want to help him."

Time passed, and one day I got a call from the friend in Meir's yeshivah. "He has an unbelievably heavy stutter," he told me. "He can't say a single word without tripping over it. You have no idea how scared he is. He knows why this is happening to him."

During one of these conversations, I told him to put Meir on the phone.

"Good morning," I said to Meir. "What's new?"

"I-I-I-I-I-I..."

I thought he was making fun of me again. I'd never heard him stutter before.

Again I heard, "I-I-I-I-I-I-I..."

I didn't say anything. I found it hard to believe that this was for real. He got out some random syllables. Cried. Said he was sorry, and that he really wanted me to forgive him. And then he made a big mistake. He said, "Listen, Co-co-co-co-hen…"

I clicked off.

I knew that this time he hadn't meant to mock me. Still, hearing him say my name that way ripped open all the old wounds.

❈   ❈   ❈

The *rosh yeshivah* started talking with me every day. He didn't pressure me. He'd say, "I'm not asking you to forgive him, but just to listen to what I have to say." He spoke words of inspiration and encouragement, telling me that we are here in this world to fix things. Stuff like that.

I'd sit with the *rosh yeshivah* during his private time. When I felt guilty, I'd burst out crying. He gave me hours of his time. He'd talk to me in *limud*, all the time building me up. He did it to become close to me, to heal me from everything I'd been through.

Due to his efforts, eventually I agreed to meet with Meir and talk with him.

I was in for a shock. I had progressed in improving my speech to a point where you could hardly tell I'd ever had a stutter. Meir's situation was much worse than any I'd experienced.

He was a shell of the person he'd once been. He couldn't finish a sentence. It didn't take me long to realize that the stutter was the least of his troubles. He'd gone from being a popular, well-liked boy to a nervous, insecure kid. I think the knowledge that what was happening to him didn't seem to have any "natural" cause but appeared to be punishment from Above tormented him.

I couldn't help but feel sorry for him.

I sat next to him listening to his broken speech. I told him I was doing everything I could to forgive him, but it would take time.

If before the meeting I'd planned on letting him have it, such thoughts disappeared the minute I saw him. There was no need.

"Look," I said to Meir, "I think I'll be able to find it in me to forgive you. So you'll know I mean it, I'm planning on sending my mother to talk to my speech therapist. She's one of the best in the country, and there's a long waiting list to get treated by her. But I'm going to ask her to help you as soon as possible."

I caught the look of surprise on his face. With great difficulty, he murmured a few words of thanks.

I'd decided to do it in stages. First I'd help him, and then later on I'd somehow find the strength to forgive him for the years of terrible suffering he'd inflicted on me.

You won't believe what happened in the next few days. We were finishing up my treatment, because by now I was talking normally. And then, at the next-to-the-last meeting, I said to Tamar, the speech therapist, "There's a new patient I want to send to you."

"Are you talking about a boy in your class?" she asked.

"No," I said, "I'm talking about Meir."

Silence. The speech therapist looked at me and said, "You're a real tzaddik. Not many boys your age would be willing to help the person who hurt them." Then she added, "Maybe send him to someone else. I'm afraid that despite your nobility of soul, it might hurt you."

"I don't think so," I said. "It's part of the reconciliation process. I think that after I help him, I'll be able to forgive him, and I'd like you to help me with this."

"Okay," she told me. "My appointment book is full, but in another week you'll be having your last treatment. *Baruch Hashem*, you speak clearly and fluently. You no longer need me. I think it will be symbolic that the minute you and I end our sessions, I'll start helping the boy who added so much anguish to your already difficult situation."

We made up to meet the following Sunday, and the next week she would begin working with Meir. I informed the *rosh yeshivah* of these plans, and he told Meir's parents. They agreed to go with Meir on Sunday two weeks later.

On Thursday, three days before my last meeting, the speech therapist's eldest son got engaged.

We were invited to the engagement party as if we were part of the immediate family. My parents and I were there, rejoicing with everyone. Tamar found the time to tell my mother that she was looking forward to her last session with me. She said that as happy a time as it would be, it would also be sad. Those were her very words.

But plans are one thing, and real life another. That very same night, the night Tamar celebrated the engagement of her eldest son, she went to sleep and never woke up. She died quietly in her sleep, the peaceful passing of a righteous woman.

No words can describe our shock and anguish. We attended the funeral, and everyone wondered who we were. Who was that family that was sobbing just as hard as the children?

Sunday rolled around, the day we were to say good-bye to the treatments. But we had already said our good-byes on Thursday.

My friend called and said Meir was in a terrible state. He felt that God was punishing him. That's what he said. First He'd given him a harsh punishment, measure for measure, and now He'd taken away the person who could help him. Meir had had such great hopes for the treatment, and now he had no hope whatsoever.

I felt bad for him. I realized that Meir had reached rock bottom. I decided to help him.

❋   ❋   ❋

I went to the *rosh yeshivah* and told him that I felt ready to forgive Meir.

He probed. Was I really sure that I wanted to forgive him completely?

"For three years he tortured you and hurt you so much. Do you really feel you can forgive him?" he asked.

I told him that I felt I could, and that I wanted to do it for the elevation of the soul of my speech therapist, Tamar.

He hugged me. "You don't know the merit you've gained."

Then he took out a text expressing forgiveness, composed by the Vilna Gaon, for me to say.

And that's what I did. I opened up the piece of paper and read what was written. I don't remember the whole thing, only a few words: "I forgive with my whole heart and soul So-and-so the son of So-and-so..." I needed to say it three times, and I did.

As soon as I finished, a huge stone rolled off my heart. I'd felt guilty for all the suffering Meir was going through, for the heavy stutter he had that was so much worse than mine had ever been. I was able to forgive him with all my heart, in part because I did it in stages.

❋　　❋　　❋

For the second time, I'm going to write, "You won't believe what happened."

The following afternoon, my friend called me up. "Let me ask you something. What have you been doing in the past couple of days?"

"Why do you ask?"

"Because starting last night, a huge change came over Meir. He's still stuttering, but at least he can talk. It's a 180-eighty degree turn, and it happened instantly."

"Yesterday I forgave him," I said.

He couldn't believe his ears. I had to tell him in detail everything that had happened, and I'm pretty sure he didn't believe that, either. Things like that just don't happen.

Within the hour, Meir's *rosh yeshivah* was at my yeshivah. He wanted to know if everything I'd said was true. He couldn't believe it. He sat across from me and my *rosh yeshivah*, who said, "It's all true. Two days ago, I gave him the Vilna Gaon's text for granting forgiveness, and the next morning, he said it. He forgave Meir completely."

"Just as Hashem is compassionate, you too must be compassionate," the *rosh yeshivah* said, referring to the mitzvah we have to emulate Hashem. He heaped praise on me and showered me with blessings. He said he'd never seen such a clear, open message from Heaven about a matter between one person and another. "It's a double message," he told me. "Both the punishment, and your forgiveness."

That's the story. The merciful, compassionate Creator of the world doesn't forgive transgressions between us and our fellowman, and He can extract a price here in this world.

If you did cause harm to another person (and I hope you didn't), run to ask his forgiveness before it's too late.

A final word: I married at a very early age. Today I work in *chinuch* and am very successful at what I do. Every year in one of the very first classes I give, I make sure to tell my students this special story. And believe me, maybe because of the story's impact, I have hardly ever encountered in all my years of teaching one of my students who deliberately hurts another. My personal story contains a powerful, unforgettable message, which is why I decided to share it with the public.

Written in memory of Tamar Berger, *a"h*, a pioneering speech therapist in the *chareidi* community in both Hebrew and Yiddish, for whom 13 Tammuz 5754 marked seventeen years since her sudden passing on the day of the engagement of her son, Rabbi Shmuel Berger, *shlita*. She left an illustrious family, and during her lifetime merited to help thousands of patients regain their ability to express themselves.

5

Dada

An unusual funeral took place a little under a year ago in Karmiel, a Jewish town midway between Akko and Tzfas.

The deceased was ninety-one years old, and her funeral procession numbered in the hundreds. Each participant considered himself family, though not one of them was even distantly related.

It wasn't a Jewish funeral, either. That's because the deceased wasn't Jewish. She was a Christian Arab by the name of Eva Abdul Kareem, and she was buried in Karmiel's non-Jewish cemetery.

If the facts sound extraordinary, that's because they are. Most of the people accompanying the deceased to her final resting place came because they wanted to hear the story.

It all began with a Jewish Lebanese family. In 1943, before the state of Israel was established, Tufik and Linda Levy, both from Beirut, were married. Two years later, their son Rafael was born, and two years after that, their daughter Sarin (Sarah). Following Sarin's birth, Linda fell ill with atherosclerosis, a disease that had no cure.

Despite her condition, Linda gave birth to twins, Maiyee and Mishleen. Three weeks later, her condition took a turn for the worse to the point where she could no longer function.

Tufik, busy with the struggle to support his family, brought in a registered nurse to care for the twins and their mother. The nurse was a Lebanese Christian Arab named Eva Abdul Kareem.

When the twins turned two, they started calling her "Dada," and the name stuck until her very last day on earth.

Dada cared for the bedridden mother and her four children. When Tufik had a heart attack and could no longer work, the family's dependence on Dada became total. Dada quit her job as a nurse to devote her life to caring for the Levy family: father, mother, and the four children.

Dada was there morning, noon, and night, serving as both mother and father. She cooked, cleaned, did the laundry, dressed the children, and most amazing of all, saw to their Jewish education.

The children attended a Christian school because that's what there was in Beirut. But Dada made sure to enroll them in a Jewish youth group that would teach them about Judaism, and she gave them a Jewish atmosphere at home. Dada fasted right along with them on Yom Kippur, and kept Shabbat and Jewish holidays, "for the sake of the children's education," as she used to say.

One day, Tufik died of a heart attack. Only three weeks later, Linda died too. The four orphans were now completely alone in Beirut. By now, few Jews remained in the city. Almost all had immigrated to America, Canada, and South America, where many assimilated. A few made their way to Israel.

Dada stayed with the four children and took them under her wing, giving up her chances to marry and raise a family of her own. She sacrificed her life for the children.

When the twins, Maiyee and Mishleen grew up, Christian families started expressing an interest in having them marry their sons. Dada fought tooth and nail to prevent it, no matter how much danger that put her in. No one understood why this

Christian woman was so stubborn about keeping those children in the Jewish religion.

"You're hurting the children," people told her. "They'll never get married. There are no Jews around for them to marry."

Where pressure and threats had left Dada unmoved, this rational argument forced her to confront the truth. But what could she do?

Without saying a word to anyone, she traveled to Belgium where she received immigration permits to Israel.

Immigration papers for the four children, that is, but not Dada. As a Christian Arab, she wasn't entitled to one.

Saying good-bye wasn't easy, but Dada explained to the children that there was no choice. She promised to do all in her power to join them in Israel.

The four Levy children were absorbed by Israel as part of the large aliya from North Africa. Maiyee and Mishleen entered a Jewish Agency institution in Netanya.

For the twins, age nineteen, adjustment was hard. It was a new country with a new language to learn – and they were alone. Everyone around them seemed to be part of a warm, extended family, while they had no one.

One day, the principal called Maiyee and Mishleen into her office and told them that a woman claiming to be their relative was looking for them. The principal looked away and then she added, "She said her name is Eva Abdul Kareem, and I think she's an Arab."

The girls didn't even take the time to answer her. "Dada!" they shouted and ran out to the gate, where they fell into the arms of the woman who had given up everything to raise them.

For the next few months, Dada lived with them in the institution. She told them that she'd gone from Lebanon to Syria and then to Jordan before finally reaching Israel.

When her tourist visa expired, again Dada was forced to separate from "her girls." Again she traveled a long route home to Lebanon through Jordan and Syria.

Maiyee and Mishleen kept in touch with Dada through letters sent to Sarin, their older sister, who was now living in Switzerland. Ten years passed without Maiyee and Mishleen seeing Dada. And then, in 1982, the First Lebanon War broke out.

It was a war with much blood spilled, many wounded and killed. To destroy the terrorist positions from which Katyusha rockets were fired on the Galilee, the Israeli government decided to push twenty-five miles into Lebanon.

Those twenty-five miles stretched to 100, until the army captured Beirut. Lebanon was destroyed, but the IDF suffered heavy losses, with over 600 soldiers dead and close to 4,000 wounded.

All communication with Dada ended. Filled with anxiety over her fate, Maiyee and Mishleen approached journalist Ehud Ya'ari, a well-connected military correspondent covering the war in Lebanon, and asked him to find out what had happened to Dada.

It took him four months before he had any information. He told the twins he'd found Dada in Khalde, a small town near Beirut's airport, staying with family. He'd told Dada about the marriages of the children she'd raised and about the children born to them. She'd nearly fainted from excitement and wouldn't let him leave until he told her everything he knew. He gave her the phone numbers and addresses of Maiyee and Mishleen and said that they were waiting anxiously for her to come to Israel, or, at the very least, call.

A few months passed, and then one day a phone call came from Beit Lechem. Dada was on the line. Yes, she had managed to get out of Lebanon, though war was still raging. She was in Beit Lechem and wanted to know how to get to them. The twins gave her directions to the central bus station in Haifa, and asked that she carry a black umbrella to help them find her.

Without the umbrella, they wouldn't have recognized her. The woman they met looked very different from the woman who had raised them. The devastating war in Lebanon had left its mark. When they'd left, she'd been a still-vibrant mother to them. Now she was a frightened old woman. She jumped at every loud sound, traumatized from the bombings she'd lived through.

Maiyee and Mishleen took her home to rest from her difficult journey. But Dada would agree to stay for only a few days. She said she was taking care of a woman who was on her deathbed, "just like your mother." She promised to return the moment the woman no longer needed her.

Due to Dada's special care, it wasn't until four years later that the woman no longer needed her. Right after that, Dada packed a suitcase and made her way to the Good Fence in Metula, on Israel's northern border with Lebanon.

It was 1986. The war had ended, but the IDF was still stuck in the Lebanese mud. Dada called and said, "I'm in Metula, and I don't want to return to Lebanon anymore."

Now began the start of the Levys' attempts to get an entry permit for her. They pulled out all stops to get her admitted to the county, and in the end, they succeeded. Dada entered Israel through the Good Fence and went straight to the home of Maiyee Lahat in Shechenya, a community twenty minutes from Karmiel.

The permit expired after a year, and the Ministry of the Interior asked Dada to leave.

The family approached Uri Lubrani, at that time coordinator of the Activities of the Israeli Armed Forces in Lebanon. Lubrani helped get Dada's permit extended for another year. At the end of that second year, they told her that nothing more could be done. She had to return to Beirut.

Another parting for Maiyee and Mishleen, no less painful than the others. Now their families joined them in tears as they said good-bye to their beloved adopted savta and accompanied her to the Good Fence, where they watched her cross through to Lebanon. They couldn't believe this was happening to them, that this woman – who had saved their lives and raised them like a real mother, even making sure they retained their Jewish identity – was being forced to leave the country.

After two weeks of frantic efforts, they managed to get her another permit, and she returned from Beirut. Family members spoke with then-Knesset Speaker Shevach Weiss and told him the story. Weiss, a Holocaust survivor, burst into tears and promised to do everything in his power to protect this special woman. He asked them to send their request in writing to several people, including the prime minister.

In their letter, they told the story of Dada's many worthy deeds, how she had rescued a Jewish family physically and spiritually. They also noted that she had no family of her own, so there was no risk of her asking to bring other family members into the country under a family unification clause or other such things. They emphasized the humanitarian aspect, for Dada had no one to help her other than "her daughters" in Israel.

The permit was renewed yearly for the next five years. One day, Dada was asked to sign papers giving up her Lebanese citizenship. She did so willingly, and a month later, she received her Israeli ID card.

For twenty-seven years Dada lived in Maiyee's home in Shechenya, surrounded by the Lahat and Masau families, both Torah and mitzvah observant.

Maiyee and Mishleen founded The Twin's Restaurant, which serves authentic Lebanese kosher food. The recipes are ones that Dada taught them back in Lebanon, plus ones they taught her in Israel.

One Tuesday, Dada died. She was ninety-one years old, an Arab Christian who was a heaven-sent agent of rescue to save four Jewish families. The four Levy children were *the only ones* in their class not to intermarry – in large part, thanks to her.

Dada was a childless woman who gave up her own personal happiness for the sake of four orphans, but she died surrounded by loved ones who considered her their beloved *savta* in all respects.

At the funeral, hundreds of people escorted her to her final resting place. No, it wasn't a Jewish funeral. No one said Kaddish, and she was buried in a Christian cemetery.

But the twins sat a "psychological *shivah*," for she was their adoptive mother, and they were forever grateful to her for making sure they stayed Jewish.

6

Put It on Ice

The story I want to tell you is about my father, who passed away a year ago in his late nineties.

My father had a company that made ice. In the forties and fifties, companies like that here in Israel sold ice to everyone. Back then, not everyone had a refrigerator, and the only way to keep fresh meat or milk or all the things we're used to refrigerating today, was with blocks of ice.

The advent of refrigerators decimated most of the market, though a few companies survived by providing ice to those who still needed it, like caterers using a hall that still didn't have refrigeration.

My father and his partner caught on at a relatively early stage that the business was melting almost as fast as ice, if not faster. They made a very smart move and went into dry ice production.

Dry ice looks like regular ice, but the two are fundamentally different. Dry ice is much colder and stays frozen a longer time than regular ice. It also doesn't actually melt. It evaporates into gas instead of turning into water.

This ice is used extensively in planes, ice skating rinks, and food shipments. The advantage of dry ice over regular ice is that it can be stored in cartons, and they don't get wet.

My father and his partner quickly became the leading manufacturers of dry ice in the country, and my childhood was spent in the shadow of the factory. My father worked from dawn till dusk. In my teens, I used to help him at the factory, at first for fun, and then for pay.

I always knew that when I grew up, I wouldn't want to work in the factory. The ice business didn't interest me. I guess there was nothing about it that warmed my heart...

What's interesting is that the children of my father's partner also stayed away from it like from fire. Or like the burn a person can get from dry ice, which is no less dangerous than a burn from fire.

We kids got married one after the other and went into various professions, while my father and his partner continued to run the factory. When they reached retirement age, no one told them they had to stop, and it didn't occur to them to say it to themselves, either. That's why they kept running the factory until they neared eighty.

At that point, I suggested to my father that he invest some of his money in a mutual fund I had invested in. I explained that since he had a lot of money in his bank account – we're talking about several millions – and since he didn't invest in real estate, he should invest in some solid stocks that would give him a good return.

At first, my father didn't want to hear about it. He said that financial advisers are heartless types who aren't interested in anything but money. I agreed with his assessment, and said that was exactly why I wanted him to meet one of them. I showed him twenty years' worth of data from my portfolio, so he could see for himself. I'd gotten very impressive returns on my money with solid, no-risk investments, while his money had been sitting in the bank earning no more than 1 percent interest annually.

I used all my persuasive talents to convince him. Eventually, my father agreed to come with me to meet the managing director of the brokerage firm I dealt with.

The director was a thirty-year-old man whose every waking moment revolved around money. There was nothing else in his life. Even his jokes were about money and investments. They were funny enough, but just to people on a certain side of the financial divide, namely, the rich side.

I think even your stories, Mr. Walder, would bore him. What does he care about suspense, pain, surprise, sadness, tears, and laughter as opposed to a stock that's going to make it big, or a company that's going under but he's going to make money on it because he has a put option. A put option means, basically, that the more the company loses, the more you stand to gain. Now you have a picture of the type of person you need to be to feel joy when thousands of other people feel…

But that's exactly why I picked him. I wasn't looking for someone with a lot of feelings to handle my money. Not at all. Emotions can lead to a lot of mistakes. He was honest and trustworthy, and besides, he had a unique perspective on life. I enjoyed listening to him and seeing him in action, but I didn't want to get too close. He'd increased my nest egg appreciably and legally, and as far as I was concerned, that's all that mattered.

During the meeting, my father expressed a lot of his reservations. The man explained to him how much he was losing by leaving his money in the bank – and believe me, it was a yearly amount equivalent to an average salary over a lifetime – as opposed to what he could make with the most risk-free, solid investment the financial advisor had to offer.

At the end of the meeting, my father said to me that he hadn't changed his mind about financial advisors, "especially this one," but nonetheless he agreed to invest a very respect- able amount in the mutual fund suggested to him.

A few years down the road, my father agreed it had been a wise move. He couldn't believe how much money he was making without working, something he'd never experienced before in his life. Still, he never forgot to make a remark or two about financial advisors.

Though the money piled up, it didn't cross my father's mind to leave the factory.

✾　　✾　　✾

One day, my father's business partner asked to bring in his son-in-law into running the factory. My father agreed without hesitation and without any stipulations. The depth of friendship between them was unusual, as was their mutual trust. The man came on board, and fit in nicely. Slowly but surely he took on more responsibility, without either of the two senior partners interfering.

Then my father's partner asked him to let the son-in-law buy shares in the company. My father agreed with this request as well, and the two of them sold stock in the company. Now the company was divided into three, with equal shares belonging to my father, his partner, and the son-in-law.

At the age of eight-seven, my father's partner had a heart attack and died at the factory, just the way he'd always dreamed of, without illness or any fuss. He just sat down, and his soul left him.

My father was devastated, though they'd both joked about it for years with a kind of black humor I found hard to understand. But when it came down to it, they weren't prepared at all. I'd never seen my father so distraught. They'd been best friends since they were kids, with never a fight between them, not even raised voices.

As if this wasn't enough, in the middle of the *shivah*, a messenger came to my father's house and handed him a letter.

My father read the letter and collapsed. It was a letter of dismissal from the factory.

He called me on the phone and I came running over. I read the letter and couldn't believe my eyes. My first thought was that it was some kind of mistake. What was going on? But my confusion quickly turned to fury. I'm considered a calm, even-keeled person. This was the first time I'd felt unbridled rage. I knew how graciously my father had agreed – by the way, after discussing it with me and getting my wholehearted approval – to take the son-in-law into the business and eventually hand over the reins to him. And then to even sell him shares in the company and turn him into a partner! And now, when the son-in-law inherited the second third, he couldn't wait more than three days to use the power given to him by my father – to fire him! It was beyond belief.

I called the son-in-law, but he wouldn't talk to me and instead referred me to his lawyer. I never thought I'd meet up with such disgraceful behavior.

My father became anxious and worried that he'd be tight for money, even though his future and that of his children was secure. Some older people lose their self-confidence for no apparent reason. He told me that he wanted to cash in his stocks because he was afraid of losing everything.

I tried to convince him not to do it, but after the double blow of losing his lifelong partner and being betrayed by the son-in-law, he wasn't in a place where he could hear me. I called up the financial advisor and said that my father wanted to cash in his stocks.

He agreed at once, and suggested that he meet with my father to discuss exactly how to liquidate such a large holding.

They met, and he showed my father the substantial returns his money was bringing in – much more than he'd promised. In a dry voice, he asked my father if the reason he wanted to cash in his portfolio had to do with dissatisfaction with the way the money was invested.

My father said that he had no complaints, but that he needed the money because he'd been fired from his job. The financial advisor blinked. It was the first time I had seen him surprised.

"Fired? How old are you, sir?"

My father didn't understand the question. To his way of thinking, nothing was more normal than an eighty-eighty-year-old man with a full-time job.

"Who fired you?" the financial advisor asked. "I thought you owned the business."

"That *shmendrik* fired me," my father said.

I gave the financial advisor a brief rundown of events. He listened, his expression revealing nothing. One eyebrow lifted when I told him about my father giving shares to the son-in-law – that was something his analytical mind could not understand. When I got to the part where my father received a note of dismissal three days after his partner's death, the financial advisor raised the other eyebrow.

In case I thought this signaled that the matter had touched his heart, or, in other words, that he had a heart, the financial advisor started asking my father questions about his factory, its production, its expenses and revenues, until finally he asked, "How much do you think the factory is worth?"

My father was surprised by the question. I thought he'd need time to calculate the price, but he had the information at his fingertips.

"My partners and I brought in an outside evaluator two years ago, and he estimated the company's worth at..." He mentioned a significant sum.

"Look," the financial advisor said, "our investment portfolio includes companies we've bought. What would happen if I offered more than the amount you mentioned? Do you think he'd agree to sell the business?"

"Why would you do something like that?" my father asked.

"Financial considerations," the financial advisor said crisply. "According to your description, I think I can maximize the company's profits to bring in greater earnings than what it's been bringing in to date."

"I don't know," my father said. "Talk to him. He owns two thirds of the company. What does this have to do with me?"

"Give me a few days," the man said. "With your permission, I'll approach him. In the meantime, leave your money where it is, because if I become the owner of the company, I'll want you to run it." After a moment of stunned silence, he added, "For professional reasons, of course. I think this new partner of yours, or to put it more accurately, the man who doesn't want to continue being your partner, doesn't know how to value your worth to the company."

My father beamed at the compliment.

The meeting ended. The financial advisor asked us to promise not to let on to the partner that we knew him.

My father left the meeting and said to me, "Forget it. I don't believe these financial advisors. Nothing's will come of it."

Here's what happened over the next few days. Employees at the brokerage firm called the partner to feel out his interest in selling the company. Then the financial advisor met with the owner and offered him a sum almost double the real value of the company.

The man didn't even try to bargain or refuse. He agreed immediately. The lawyers drew up agreements and at this stage, a problem arose: the third still owned by my father.

The financial advisor met with the owner of the two-thirds of the shares, who was very apprehensive about the meeting. He realized the whole sale was in jeopardy. But the financial advisor reassured him by saying that, based on his in-depth assessment of the business, he saw no need to make changes in the way the company was run. In fact, one of his conditions was that both managers continue to run it as before, especially the elderly one, due to his extensive contacts locally and abroad, and his many years of successful management of the company.

The partner expressed his full agreement, making no mention of the dismissal letter he'd sent to that very same elderly man.

The financial advisor then said that he wanted a contract drawn up stating that for the next five years there would be no change in the management of the company.

The man quickly promised him this, and right after the meeting, called my father and told him that the dismissal letter had been sent without his knowledge, that his lawyer had sent it, and that my father should consider it null and void. He also said he wanted to sign a new contract with him to continue to run the company for at least another five years.

My father happily agreed, without taking him to task for what had happened. That very evening, they both signed, with lawyers present, an agreement ensuring my father's continued employment in his position for the next five years.

The partner then called the financial advisor, who said he was tied up and wouldn't be available for another week.

The partner waited anxiously for the week to pass. The financial advisor invited him to an upscale restaurant, and the man was in seventh heaven. They ate a meal fit for a king, with expensive wines and a rich menu. After desert, the financial advisor took out his credit card, paid for the meal, and stood up.

Suddenly, he sat back down. "By the way," he said, "we made further inquiries and we've decided that we're not interested in the business. Anyway, nice meeting you."

With that, he left.

My father returned to the factory. The partner didn't even tell him to what heights his dreams had soared or how suddenly they had crashed. They continued working alongside each other as if nothing had happened.

As for me, at my next meeting with the financial advisor, I thanked him from the bottom of my heart. He didn't understand what I was grateful for.

"I was looking to make a profitable deal, and in the end I reached the conclusion that it wasn't a good idea. What's there to thank me for?"

I looked in his eyes, and for the first time saw a flicker of humanity.

"It's your father," he said. "He's everything I'll never be. He's a real man. He worked hard all his life to earn money, and didn't play with other people's money. My father was like that too. You're the same way. I felt a moral responsibility to do what I did. He touched my heart, your father...the heart you always say I don't have. And truthfully, the heart whose existence I myself had forgotten."

The moment of weakness and emotion passed as quickly as it had appeared. The mask returned to his face, and he said, "Especially since it didn't cost me a cent." He shook his head ruefully. "Except for dinner at the restaurant."

My father continued to run the company until the day he died at a ripe old age, yet every time we'd talk about the financial advisor, he'd say, "I told you they can't be trusted!"

7

The Wedding Present

This is a confession of sorts.

I'm not proud of what I did. Actually, I'm very ashamed of it and would rather forget all about it. But telling the story is part of my repentance. Confession and repentance go well together.

It all took place not that long ago. I was a *yeshivah bachur*, started going out, and quickly got engaged to a wonderful seminary girl.

My father always said there's a huge difference between the wedding preparations for a boy and those for a girl. The girl needs to run from the seamstress to the wig salon and take care of a thousand other things, while all the boy has to do is walk into a few stores to get a suit, shoes, hat, and tie, and that's it.

Okay, so my father belongs to the previous generation. He doesn't know that in our generation buying a hat is a process that wouldn't put a bride to shame (or maybe it would... depending on who was doing the embarrassing and who was being embarrassed). Finding the right suit demanded a trek of dozens of miles, and the tie was a story without end because of the unbelievable range of choices. Sometimes it felt like every

Chinaman made a tie, which meant at least a billion ties to choose from. Anyway, it's a different generation. People have changed – some of them, at least. There are still a lot of guys who treat superficialities as just that, superficial.

I wanted to wear an expensive suit to my wedding. Something extravagant. Don't ask me why. People get these crazy ideas, and this was mine. Everyone in my yeshivah knew about it. It became a catchphrase in yeshivah: "Like the suit Shimon's going to buy for his wedding…"

Three weeks before the wedding, I went to a very expensive district in Tel Aviv where I'd heard they sell suits to the rich and famous. I knew the prices would be sky-high, but I didn't know to what extent.

I looked around a little, and found a suit that was just what I wanted. It was an amazing suit, and looked like it had been tailor-made for me. I knew right then and there that this was the suit I was going to wear to my wedding.

"This is it," I said to the salesman.

"Great," he said. "You've had the good fortune to choose one of our less expensive models. It's only six thousand shekels."

"What?"

"Yes, you're right to be surprised," he said. "We carry models like this for regular people at an affordable price."

"Are you feeling okay?" I said. "Six thousand shekels is an affordable price to you?"

He looked at me like I'd landed from outer space. "Listen, kid," he said, "this isn't the flea market. You're in the most expensive shopping district in the country. Suit prices start at twenty thousand shekels, and I don't want to tell you where they end, because I don't need an ambulance siren blaring its way to the store."

I looked at the price tags. You may not believe it, but there are people who spend eighty thousand shekels on a suit. When they said "rich and famous," I guess I missed the real meaning.

"Sorry," I said. "It's not for me."

I got out of there fast, and, to be on the safe side, I fled the whole shopping district. There's a limit to how much disappointment a person can take.

The next two weeks found me slightly depressed. I know a lot of people are going to be saying, "That guy's got a problem. All he can think about is a suit?" Maybe they're right, but everyone's got his own craziness, and mine was to wear *the* suit. I have to say that I'm not one of those guys who's busy all the time with externals or who's looking for instant gratification. In yeshivah, I sat and *shteiged* and didn't get involved in *shtussim*. I have a weakness for aesthetics, but I never took it too far. I had only one dream: to be an elegant, handsome groom, just like it says, "Like a bridegroom leaving his wedding canopy, joyful as a champion going the distance."

The week before the wedding, I bought a suit that was nice but very average. You know – the kind I wore as a *bachur*. I felt bad that after telling everyone about my dream suit I was going to appear at my wedding in a standard suit like those worn by every *chasan*.

Now we're getting to the part I'm ashamed of.

A day before the wedding, I went back to the store. I told the salesman that I was having a hard time deciding about the suit and that my wife wanted to see it on me first.

"I'll give you a check as security," I told him. "Worse comes to worst, I'll bring it back in a day or two."

The gracious salesman agreed right away. He didn't even ask for the check. He just asked for my contact info, boxed the suit, and gave it to me.

I walked away. I don't know what was going through my mind. I convinced myself that since I was going to return the suit, it wasn't really stealing. I remembered that when I was a kid, a friend told me they'd bought nice clothes, had a professional photographer take some shots, and then they'd returned the clothes under some pretext. At the time, I thought it was a funny prank. Later on, I realized that it had an element of theft in it, but the idea stayed with me.

Let me say right now that I'm a guy who stays far away from anything that might even remotely be considered stealing, including stealing someone's sleep, but suddenly, here I was giving myself permission to do it.

The wedding arrived. I stood under the *chuppah* in my expensive suit, feeling like a king. All my friends complimented me, saying, "Shimon, you're really a person who 'says and does, speaks and fulfills.'" Good thing they didn't continue with the rest of the verse, "for all his words are true and just," because that suit was one big untruth and injustice.

From the *chuppah*, I walked to the *yichud* room, and just before we left it to rejoin the celebration, I told my new wife that I wanted to change out of the expensive suit I'd rented so it wouldn't get ruined by the dancing. I stepped out for a minute, changed into a different suit, also a new one, and carefully returned the suit to its box. I went back to the *yichud* room, and together we left for the dancing.

The wedding was perfect – filled with joy, excitement, lots of guests, and my friends' energized dancing. At the end of the wedding, I felt that everything had gone smoothly. I'd stood there under the *chuppah* in that millionaire's suit, and I hadn't damaged it in the slightest. Now I could return it as I'd promised, and everything would be okay.

The day after the wedding, I sent my brother to the tailor to take out the stitches he'd put in to shorten the pants, and to return the suit to the store. I told him to tell the salesman I was sorry, but my wife didn't like the suit.

My brother gave me a strange look. He made no comment, but I could see that he knew exactly what was going on. He and I are very close. We always help each other and cover for each other, just as he was doing then.

At the first *sheva berachos*, I asked him, "How did it go?"

"Everything's okay," he answered me.

"Did he notice?" I asked.

"Nope. He didn't say a thing. Everything's okay. Be happy."

I saw he wasn't being completely open with me, though he did his best to hide it.

❋   ❋   ❋

The next day, my wife and I found the time to open our gifts. We began with the envelopes. It was a lot of fun, sort of like scratching off lottery tickets, only here there were hundreds of them…all winners. You look at the name and say, "Hmmm. I wonder how much he gave." You open the envelope and are amazed. "Wow. That's nice of them. I can't believe it. Look how much they gave." Or, "Good," or, "Hmmm." And rarely, "He should live and be well." The cheapskates get all the blessings. You never thought of that one, did you?

I opened the envelopes and my wife wrote down, in her beautiful handwriting, the name of the giver and the amount given. We did that so our parents would have some idea what their friends had given, both so they could express their thanks and also to prevent a situation where they'd inadvertently give less to their friend's child at his wedding – or, God forbid, more.

We finished the list and totaled up the gifts. It came to a nice amount of money, and at that night's *sheva berachos*, I gave my father the list. He'd make a copy and give it to the other side.

My father glanced at the list and looked worried. He went over it again and again, and it looked like something was bothering him.

"What's the matter, Abba?" I asked.

He hesitated, but finally said, "There's no gift here from Meshulam. Is it possible he bought something?"

Just so you understand, in our family, the expression "bought something" is just about the worst thing you can say of someone, unless that "something" is a washer or dryer.

"I'll double-check," I said, feeling hurt for my father that Meshulam would have "bought something" instead of giving a nice fat check.

Meshulam was a young guy with nothing going for him when my father first met him. My father took him under his wing, married him off, and gave him his start in business. Meshulam is now set up and doing quite well. Not that my father needed his money, but from him more than anyone, he expected it.

When we got home, we sat for a long time opening presents. There were a lot, but not even one from Meshulam.

Meshulam joined us for the last *sheva berachos*. He had a strange expression on his face, and kept looking at my father in a funny way. My father didn't know what was behind it.

Meshulam moved close to my father and stayed there for a few minutes before saying anything to him. I was nearby when he asked my father, "Did you get my present?"

"Did you give a present?" my father asked.

"Of course I did," Meshulam said. "I gave an envelope with cash."

"I was getting worried," my father said as a stone rolled off his chest. "I thought you were mad at me or something."

"I didn't understand what was going on either," Meshulam said. "I put in a nice amount, and it seemed strange to me that you didn't say anything."

"First of all, I'm glad you came to clarify. Now we just have to find out where it is," my father said. "Is it possible that it was stolen from the safe?"

"No," Meshulam said. "I myself handed it to your son just before the *chuppah*. He put the envelope in his jacket pocket. I saw him do it."

When he said that, it was like, "...and they covered Haman's face..."

Haman, in this case, was me.

I remembered exactly when I'd put the envelope in my pocket. I remembered being surprised that Meshulam hadn't put it in the safe, but I assumed that he wanted to give it to me personally. I took it and forgot about it.

And the suit was...

"Tonight you'll look in the suit pocket and everything will be okay," my father said.

"Okay," I said, though I knew nothing was okay. The suit had been returned to the store, and my father knew nothing about it...and I certainly wasn't going to be the one to tell him.

The final blow came when Meshulam said, "Don't take it lightly. There's six thousand shekels in cash."

As if from afar, I heard my father say, "Are you crazy? Why so much?" But to me, it was like I'd been hit on the head with a sledgehammer. I know you won't believe this. It sounds like I'm making it up. But the amount of money Meshulam gave me was exactly the price of the suit.

The story's still not over. The next day, I was there at the store when it opened. "Do you remember me?" I asked the salesman.

"Sure I remember you," he said. "You're the one who got sticker shock over the six thousand shekel suit."

"Uh, actually not," I said. "I thought maybe I'd buy it after all. Can you show it to me?"

"What a shame," he said. "Someone bought it yesterday afternoon. But don't worry. We expect to get in an identical suit tomorrow."

I felt dizzy.

"Someone bought it?" I heard myself say.

"Yes, but it's not a problem. Tomorrow we're getting in the exact same suit. You know what? I'll try to have them bring it this afternoon. How's that?"

"Okay. We'll see," I said gloomily, realizing I was doomed. I'd lost six thousand shekels *and* the suit I hadn't bought. *You deserve it*, I thought. *You really deserve it.*

I said good-bye and left the store wondering what I was going to tell my father and Meshulam. How had I gotten myself into such a mess?

"Hey, kid," I heard the salesman call.

I turned around.

He was standing there holding…a thick envelope.

"You left something in the suit," he said with a laugh. "Don't worry. I realized what you were up to as soon as your brother returned the suit. I must say, you returned it in perfect condition."

You can imagine how uncomfortable I felt at that moment.

"I didn't know what to do with the six grand," he said. "I had the suit, and I realized you'd worn it to some event, but still, that didn't warrant a fine of six thousand shekels for one night."

I didn't say anything.

"What did you wear it to?"

"A wedding," I said.

"Whose? Someone in your family?"

"Mine."

"Yours? Then you get a mazel tov."

"Forget it," I said. "I feel rotten."

"You should," he said. "But listen to the plan. I'll peel off six hundred shekels for the rental, and I'll give you the envelope. How does that sound to you?"

"No," I said, making a quick decision. "I have to pay for what I did. Keep the six thousand, and I'll take the suit. It'll teach me a lesson."

He thought a little and then said, "Nope. You just got married. You made a mistake, and you paid for it by suffering pangs of remorse. Let's make a deal. Here's what you do. Take the money, but tell this story, without using your name, of course. It'll give people a message. If you do that, I'll consider the matter closed."

He gave me the money, we said good-bye, and the first thing I did was to call you, Mr. Walder, and tell you the story.

I learned that nothing's gained from being dishonest. It might not seem that way at first, like with what happened to me, but it's true.

I'm building my home, and I know that no matter what happens, it will be a home built on Torah, a home of trust based on halachah, moral integrity, truth, and justice. As far as I'm concerned, that was the biggest and best wedding present I got. Double meaning.

8

An American Soldier in Meah Shearim

The person writing to you, Mr. Chaim Walder, is the Yerushalmi Yid. Maybe you've forgotten about me a little because it's been a few months since I've written to you, but don't be hurt. There are plenty of reasons for it, mostly because I've been busy from morning till night.

Should you ask what a Jew who's almost one hundred years old has to be so busy with, I'll tell you. A Jew who's one hundred years old has so many grandchildren, great-grandchildren, and great-great-grandchildren (whose number I don't want to mention because I'm afraid of *ayin hara*) that they fill his whole day and half the night.

But I've put off telling you this story far too long, the story about the visit my wife and I made to the American consul in Jerusalem in 1984.

To remove any doubts you might have, I have never set foot in the United States. Which is not such a big deal, because I have never set foot outside Jerusalem, except for a few important trips, weddings and such, including that trip to Haifa that I told you about at the beginning of our shared journey. I think I can use that expression, given the number of my stories that have appeared in your books.

Anyway, one morning I came back from davening and announced to my wife that we were going to the American consul.

"What business do you have with the American consul?" she asked suspiciously.

"Come and see," I told her.

My wife is used to me taking her to all sorts of places, so all she said was, "After you."

Since this story took place thirty years ago, when we were both younger, only seventy or so, we walked from Meah Shearim to Nablus Road where the U.S. Consulate General is located.

We arrived at the gate to the consulate. Quite a few guards were standing around because it's an Arab neighborhood and the consulate didn't exactly gain any fans for the United States, especially at that time, which was during the first intifada.

As soon as we got there, we were surrounded by burly guards. They spoke English, a language I don't really understand, mostly because it has so few Yiddish words in it. All I knew how to say was "ambassador." My wife just used her Yiddish to shout at them to let us in. I didn't try to stop her, because I knew that they knew Yiddish like I knew English, which allowed for open conversation between the two sides without fear of hurting anyone's feelings or what have you.

Only a few minutes passed before a patrol car pulled up and out came a policeman who looked to be around fifty years old.

He came over to me and said, "Reb Yid, what brings you here?"

"I want to meet with the ambassador, Shmuel Lewis," I told him.

"The ambassador's name is Samuel Lewis," he said, "and he's located in Tel Aviv, not here."

"I know the ambassador's office is in Tel Aviv, because the United States doesn't have an embassy in Jerusalem. But he's here today, and I came to talk to him."

The policeman went over to the guards and exchanged a few words with them in English. He came back to me and asked, "Tell me something. How did you know the ambassador is here today?"

"Come visit the Zupnik *mikveh* every day and you'll know everything too," I said to him.

He laughed, so I knew right then and there that if he got my meaning, he was on our side.

"Look," he said, "they're very nervous because there's a plan to move the U.S. Embassy to Jerusalem and the Neturei Karta people are working hard to prevent it. They've received orders to watch out for people who look like you."

"I know the whole story," I said. "The seventh council of Neturei Karta already sat with the Jordanian parliament and they issued a joint proclamation about it in a sharply worded letter to the United Nations. And this is a good opportunity for me to speak with Shmuel, the ambassador. I need a small favor from him, and in exchange, I'll talk in Zupnik about cooling down all this opposition."

My wife was looking at me in astonishment. Her husband from Meah Shearim was suddenly talking like a diplomat on a secret mission.

Mr. Chaim Walder, before I continue, I must tell you that I made up all those political statements I told the policeman and that my wife overheard. The truth is, I'm not a representative of or even the president of the Neturei Karta, for many good reasons, primarily because there is no such position. It's just a few Yerushalmis who are trying to earn a living and think that joining up with the Arabs, the Jordanians, and the PLO is like opening a small guesthouse. All of Meah Shearim knows that they're nothing more than a dog who barks but doesn't bite and that they're not even worth the ink it takes to print their names. Most people in the neighborhood strongly disapprove of their way of earning a living by joining up with Jew haters, but most of the community treats them with indif- ference. Because earning a living is earning a living, and in Yerushalayim no one looks down on people who tan hides in the marketplace, especially if they hate Zionism, which is not exactly admired by us in the neighborhood.

The reason I made all those statements was in the hope that they would let me meet the ambassador with the Jewish- sounding name of Shmuel Lewis so that I could ask him for a small favor.

The policeman went back to the guards and explained a few things to them. Their angry looks slowly gave way to looks of admiration. One of them spoke into his walkie-talkie in English, and it seemed to me that he was going to let me go in.

In the meantime, the policeman told us that he had passed on my message and had reassured them that I wouldn't make an attempt on the life of the ambassador. He said he personally vouched for me that I presented no security risk. He even offered to accompany me so that he could serve as translator between the ambassador and me.

I didn't know how he could take responsibility for me when even I was reluctant to do so, but naturally I didn't share my views about this with him out of fear that he'd regret his offer and shirk the responsibility.

The policeman himself solved my problem. "I remember you," he told me. "Exactly a year ago you went to Prime Minister Shamir and asked him to do a favor for some postman in your neighborhood. They're still talking about it, and at every security briefing of the Shabak (Israel Security Agency), you'll hear someone say, "How did that *chareidi* from Meah Shearim get in to see the prime minister? He knocked and walked in!"

❀   ❀   ❀

Within five minutes, they gave us a permit. We walked inside the consulate, and were taken to the consul's fancy office. And there, exactly as I'd overheard in Zupnik, sat the honorable ambassador, Shmuel Lewis.

I went right up to him, shook his hand, and said, "My dear Reb Shmuel, I came to talk to you as one Jew to another."

The policeman translated what I'd said, and they exchanged a few sentences, after which the policeman said to me sheepishly that Sam Lewis was happy I'd come, but he wasn't Jewish.

Naturally, I was disappointed with this piece of information, but I said as diplomatically as possible, "Okay, then I'm pleased to meet you, and I came to talk to you as one Jew to a goy."

The policeman started to translate, but when he got to the part "as one Jew to…" he got stuck, and the ambassador filled in the rest, "…to a goy," and started to laugh.

I took that as my opportunity to talk about the matter I'd come for, pausing after every sentence so the policeman could translate.

❊   ❊   ❊

"We have a family of converts living in Meah Shearim," I said to the ambassador. "Converts are goyim…like you… who became Jews. I want you to know, Mr. Ambassador, that it's very hard for a gentile to become a Jew. A lot of obstacles are put in his way – not like with the Christians, who want to make everyone just like them."

The policeman translated carefully, got stuck a little, but the ambassador encouraged him to translate what I said word for word and seemed to be enjoying the whole thing.

"As hard as it is to join the Jewish people, it's much harder to become part of *chareidi* society. And as hard as it is to become part of *chareidi* society, it's a hundred times harder to join Meah Shearim and Neturei Karta."

The policeman translated, and the ambassador started to get very interested.

"The family I'm talking about has been living in Meah Shearim for ten years and is fully integrated into the community. They look and dress just like us, and they're highly respected."

Here's where my wife put in her two cents. "Let's see how respected they are when they start with *shidduchim*."

I was hoping the policeman would refrain from translating that sentence, but my hopes were in vain. The ambassador burst out laughing.

"Anyway," I said, "to get to the point, everything was going along smoothly until last Purim. Last Purim, the mother of this family prepared a special costume for her eight-year-old son. Now, you should know, Mr. Ambassador, that most people dress up on Purim as they really are. People put on *shtreimels* out of cotton instead of real *shtreimels,* or paste on a long, long, long beard instead of a long beard, or wear a huge white *kippah* instead of a large white *kippah*. But children sometimes dress up as Haman or Achashverosh or Bigsan and Teresh and all kinds of characters."

The policeman got mixed up with the translation, but somehow managed to explain to the ambassador that these were evil characters from the *Tanach.*

"I'm coming to the story, Reb Shmuel, I mean Mr. Ambassador. And then the wife of the convert made her first mistake since converting. A mistake that might have been forgiven everywhere else in the world, but not by the Neturei Karta in Yerushalayim. She dressed up her son as an American soldier! Do you understand, Mr. Ambassador, what that means? I see that you do understand, but why are you laughing? Believe me, nothing funny came out of it. Her son was immediately 'discharged' from the Talmud Torah and told he couldn't 'return to base' unless his parents first came to talk to the 'commanding officer.' And now he's been sitting home for a week. His parents are afraid to go there because they have no explanation why, out of all the costumes in the world, they chose to dress up their son as a soldier. I've seen their pain these past few days, and I can't sleep at night.

"So last night as I tossed and turned, I remembered that I heard in Zupnik that the Jewish ambassador Shmuel Lewis was coming to the consulate to discuss moving the embassy to Jerusalem. Everyone was laughing, saying that anyone who wanted a job as 'foreign minister' of the Zupnik-goers could declare himself to be just that and have his picture taken in Jordan and at the United Nations and with everyone who hates Jews.

"That's when the idea suddenly came to me that I could use your visit here to help poor Moishe, the boy who dressed up as a soldier, and his whole family, which is in danger of being ostracized and banished from the community."

"How can I help?" Mr. Lewis asked.

"You'll go to his house and thank him for dressing up as an American soldier, and we'll somehow connect that with his father's request not to move the American embassy to the Zionist capital, and he'll be transformed instantly from an outcast to a superhero."

The ambassador was no longer laughing. He looked serious. I knew that what I was asking of him was no simple matter. "I know it's not an easy thing, Mr. Ambassador, but I thought to approach you as one Jew to…to another human being. Come, visit them, give him an American flag, and say that you came to find out more about the Neturei Karta. You don't have to say a thing about the embassy. Leave it to me. I'll go to Zupnik and make sure there are plenty of rumors. What's it to you? It's only a five-minute drive from here."

The ambassador seemed to enjoy the story. He excused himself for a moment to consult with someone, and then he returned, wearing a suit jacket, and said, "Let's go. You're coming with me in my car."

That's how my wife and I wound up getting a ride in the ambassador's luxurious limousine. Security vehicles drove in front of and behind us, with a police car driven by the policeman who had translated for me bringing up the end of the procession. The whole convoy headed straight for Meah Shearim.

Naturally, a convoy like that in Meah Shearim draws 90 percent of the neighborhood's residents. We got out of the car at the home of Moishe's family, the ambassador went up the stairs, presented the father of the family with a modest gift from the United States government, and asked to have his picture taken with Moishe wearing the clothes of an American soldier.

He pinned on the uniform U.S. medals he'd brought from the embassy, and the two of them went out onto the balcony to be photographed.

The ambassador shook hands and then disappeared, leaving me to prepare the father for what he had to say.

I myself went outside and said that thanks to the father of the family, all of whom were Americans by birth, who dressed up his son as an American soldier and wrote a moving letter to the U.S. ambassador pleading with him not to move the embassy to Yerushalayim, peace between two peoples was promoted, and there was a chance the plan would be canceled.

It goes without saying that the family that had been ostracized and banished turned into neighborhood heroes. The principal of the Talmud Torah apologized to Moishe's parents for his terrible mistake and said he couldn't understand how he had failed to see the American medals on Moishe's costume.

Several months later, a decision was made not to move the embassy. Believe me, Mr. Walder, not a single one of the residents failed to credit the family of converts, and their son Moishe especially.

I'm the only one who has some doubt about the family's contribution to the decision not to move the embassy, but of course I refrain from expressing this doubt to anyone, and I hope my wife does the same.

✤   ✤   ✤

The family of converts no longer lives in Meah Shearim. They moved to a different city and succeeding in erasing all traces of their past as converts.

A few months ago, a man stopped his car next to me on my way to the Kosel and offered me a ride.

"Where to?" I asked him.

"Wherever you want," he answered me.

"Are you a taxi driver?"

"No. I just want to give you a ride."

"Why?" I asked.

"Don't you recognize me?"

"Are you one of my great-grandchildren? How am I supposed to recognize you? I have over two hundred of them!"

"No, I'm not your great-grandchild. I'm Moishe. The American soldier. I'm thirty-eight now, and I'm soon going to be marrying off my daughter. I've never forgotten how you rescued me with your crazy idea. You saved my life. Instead of being ostracized and banished, you turned me into a hero. I owe you."

I was very happy to hear this. "But we owe you a lot more," I said.

"For what?" he asked.

"Thanks to you, they still haven't moved the American embassy to Yerushalayim."

9

Peace at Any Price

My story is about a short trip that continues to this very day. It's the trip I make twice weekly from Jerusalem to Tel Aviv for my jewelry business. I have a car, but I'd rather take the direct bus that stops not far my home and leaves me off right in front of the Diamond Exchange in Ramat Gan.

Traveling by bus is an interesting experience, because every bus contains a whole world of people with varying ideas, outlooks, and backgrounds, all lumped together for a limited amount of time. Usually, people prefer to keep to themselves and not talk to their fellow passengers. All it takes, though, is for one person to break the silence. That starts a chain of comments that pulls people out of their box. And since there is usually at least one passenger like that, the trip tends to become interesting. Or irritating, depending on your viewpoint.

One day, I got on the bus as usual and sat in the fourth row on the left. Following me was another *frum* man, obviously a *ba'al teshuvah*, who sat in the second row on the right.

The bus started moving, and I opened a pocket Mishnah.

Some fifteen minutes later, one of the passengers walked to the front of the bus. He didn't look like your usual bus passenger. He had that aura of wealth and status that you can spot a mile away. It's more than dress. It's a certain way of walking and talking, a certain look. Mostly, I would say, it's a commanding presence.

This man now said to the bus driver, "Sir, you gave me thirty-one shekels in change. I think you mistakenly thought I gave you a fifty-shekel bill, but I gave you a *hundred*."

"Why are you remembering this now, mister?"

"Because I was looking through my wallet and I saw that there was no fifty there, which brought me to the simple conclusion that I never got it from you."

"Maybe the exact opposite happened. Maybe you got back a *one*-hundred-shekel bill in addition to the thirty-one shekels in change." His tone said, *Who is this nudnik?*

"No, sir. My wallet is full of two-hundred-shekel bills. If you had given me one-hundred-shekel bill, I'd see it."

"There nothing I can do about what you're saying," the driver said. "I work for a living. If every passenger came and told me what you're telling me, I'd be broke."

The man started to get angry. He wasn't going to give in. In the heat of the argument, suddenly I noticed the *ba'al teshuvah* shift in his seat and look around surreptitiously, as if he were hiding something. I suspected him of wanting to do something on the sly.

I closed my eyes, feigning sleep, but left them open a crack so that I could keep an eye on him.

Just as I'd suspected, he put his hand into his back pocket, took something out of it, and swiftly transferred whatever it was to the other hand. Suddenly I saw what it was: a fifty-shekel bill. Again his eyes darted this way and that, checking to see that no one was watching, and then he pretended to go to sleep and... dropped the bill on the floor of the bus.

Now I had his number. This guy had picked the pocket of the other passenger, like he'd probably done plenty of times in his past, and now he was either afraid of the bus's security camera or he was sorry he'd done it.

Okay. Now I knew I had a role to play in this drama. I needed to "find" the lost money.

I pretended to wake up. I listened for half a minute to the strident, angry voices, including the passenger's threats to go to the police and his demand that the driver drop him off at the nearest police station. That's when I called out, "Excuse me, mister, but did this fall out of your wallet?"

"Nothing fell –" he began, but then he looked to where I was pointing. "There it is. I don't believe it." He bent over to pick up the money, and went right back to the driver, full of apologies. "I'm very sorry for this misunderstanding. But I was right. I *did* lose fifty shekels. I was wrong to blame you, though, and I ask your forgiveness."

The driver was happy to put the unpleasantness behind him. The last thing he needed was to have a passenger complain about him. Even if the complaint was dismissed, the Egged bus company keeps track of passenger complaints and will promote a driver whose record is clean over one who's had a complaint made against him, even if the complaint was dismissed.

The passenger made his way back to his seat. I wanted to say something about the arrogance and speed with which he falsely accused a working man, but I kept my mouth shut. He looked too distinguished for me to say anything. If you ask me, that's why none of my fellow passengers commented either. And there you have another one of the numerous benefits of belonging to the wealthy aristocracy. They never make a mistake, and even if they do, no one will take them to task for it.

A few minutes later, the *ba'al teshuvah* started to look at me. I avoided making eye contact, but I sensed that he was still looking my way. In a swift movement, he stood up and walked over to me.

"Okay with you if I sit here?" he asked, pointing to the empty seat next to me.

I nodded, but I was taking no chances. My right hand slid over my wallet to protect it. I kept my eyes on his hands. Say what you will, but I'd seen something none of the other passengers had.

He sat down and started right in talking. "So, did you see what happened?"

"Uh-huh," I said noncommittally. It was the most pareve uh-huh you've ever heard, the kind that usually stops a conversation in its tracks.

"What did you see?"

Now he was giving me the once over.

"I saw what happened," I told him.

"You saw me throw down the money, didn't you?" he surprised me by saying.

I considered denying it, but on second thought, I didn't owe him anything. I had tried to be nice by not revealing that I'd seen what I'd seen, but if he insisted… "Yes, I saw everything," I said.

"Do you know why I did it?"

"Why did you do it?" I asked, though I already knew the answer.

"Because my *rav* says that for shalom it's worth giving up all the money in the world," he said. "I saw a fight, and I said to myself, now you can be like Aharon, who loved peace and ran after it. And believe me, I'm no Moshe or Aharon."

"Ha," I laughed politely, inside laughing even more at how this petty thief thought he'd rob me of my senses. I wanted to tell him that Aharon would stop fights that weren't started by him, but I didn't say that, because I didn't know what else he knew how to do besides picking pockets.

"Do you know that this is all the money I have on me?" he asked me.

Now he was going to try to get me to give him a donation.

"I used my bus ticket to pay for the ride, and those fifty shekels were going to buy lunch for me and my wife. But I gave them up without hesitation for the sake of peace."

"You're really something," I said insincerely.

"Don't worry," he said. "My *rav* said that you never lose out by sacrificing for peace. You'll see. Me and my wife will have a meal much better than any I could have bought us."

"I'm sure of it," I said, though I was sure of exactly the opposite, and to tell you the truth, this was the first time in my life I'd even been interested in what was on someone else's plate.

He kept on talking and talking, but I tuned out. I couldn't wait until we reached my stop.

But then something happened that changed the whole picture.

The first passenger made his way up to the driver.

"How can I help you, sir?" the driver asked him.

"Listen, there's a bit of a mystery here," the man said.

"What now?" the driver asked impatiently. "You dropped a fifty-shekel bill and you found it. What's your problem?"

"My problem is that I found the fifty shekels you gave me. It was folded up in my ID card holder. The fifty shekels that fell must belong to someone else."

Forty passengers were shocked speechless. One passenger was not only shocked but embarrassed.

That passenger was me.

I'd spent the whole ride suspecting the fellow still sitting next to me. I was certain he'd snatched those fifty shekels, but now the truth was out. I felt ashamed of having suspected the poor innocent guy next to me.

I decided to do something. "I know who it belongs to," I declared. Everyone looked at me.

I stood up and announced, "These fifty shekels belong to the man sitting next to me. He saw you arguing, and to make peace, he gave up his last fifty shekels, which was supposed to buy lunch for him and his wife, all so that the two of you wouldn't fight with each other."

The surprise was total, for the distinguished-looking gentleman most of all.

He came over to us. "Is what he said true?"

"Yes," the man sitting next to me said.

"What made you do something like that?"

"Because my *rav* said that nothing is greater than peace and that it's worth all the money in the world to make peace. He also promised me that no one ever loses out from making peace. And here you go. Now that you've found the fifty shekels, you'll return it to me, and I'll buy lunch for me and my wife. I did a mitzvah, and I didn't lose a thing."

"Who said I'll give you back the fifty shekels?"

A flash of anger flickered across the man's face, but quickly vanished. "Listen, do whatever you want. Even if you don't give it back to me, God will repay me. If I gave up fifty shekels so that you wouldn't fight with the driver, I'm willing to give up even more so that you won't fight with me."

The man laughed. "You're not going to get fifty shekels from me," he said. "You're going to get *five thousand shekels* from me. Not only that, call up your wife and tell her you're taking her out to the most expensive *glatt kosher* restaurant in town at my expense. How does that sound?"

"Sounds good," the *ba'al teshuvah* said, shooting me a triumphant look. "Didn't I tell you my *rav* said I wouldn't lose out?"

There was one more stop to go before I had to get off. The wealthy man identified himself. He was the owner of one the largest insurance companies in the country. He said he hadn't ridden on a bus in years, but his driver was delayed and he hadn't been able to get a taxi, so he'd decided for the first time in decades, according to him, to take the bus.

"It wasn't the fifty shekels," he explained. "I'm very sensitive to people trying to take advantage of me. The minute I think someone's trying to trick me, I stand up for my rights."

"That's okay," the *ba'al teshuvah* quipped. "That's why you're rich and we aren't."

Everyone laughed.

The bus reached Arlozorov Street, the last stop, and all the remaining passengers got off. The rich man gave the *ba'al teshuvah* a check for five thousand shekels and asked for his phone number. Then he gave him another five hundred shekels "for a meal fit for a king – and keep the change."

The *ba'al teshuvah* called his wife. "Udel!" he shouted into his cell phone. "Remember how I told you about giving in for the sake of shalom? No, I'm not talking about *shalom bayis* right now..."

10

The Captive

You probably get lots of letters from people telling you their stories, but I'm certain you've never gotten one like mine.

It took me a few nights to write it. You'll find out why I wrote it when you get to the end. And the end, at least right now, is not a good one. Actually, I can't even call it an end.

I'm seventeen. What kind of story can a boy of seventeen possibly have to tell? Well, the story takes place over the past four years, but to me, it feels like a lifetime.

Our family isn't religious. My parents have almost no connection to religion – not Shabbos, not prayer, and not keeping kosher. We're considered well off, and we live in a small town that's very well-off. My family owns a successful factory. I had everything.

I attended public schools with my friends. Nothing in our lives connected us to religion in any way.

Guess what? It was your stories that did it. One day in junior high, a kid brought into class a magazine put out by Hidabroot. In it was a sad story about a soldier who was killed in the Lebanon war, leaving behind a young son. His wife married a doctor who raised the boy like a father, but made sure to keep alive the memory of the deceased father. He hung pictures of the father over the boy's bed and told the boy stories about him. The story ended with the boy's wedding.

A week later, there was a funny story about a chassid whose hat rolled away and lots of notes fell out of it or something like that. Anyway, I got into it. Practically the whole class did too.

But I took it a step further. I started to listen to all kinds of lectures, mostly those of Hidabroot. As a bar mitzvah boy, I started to read all kinds of stuff about Judaism, and somehow I got to Rabbi Zamir Cohen.

Rabbi Cohen gave me a lot of his time and attention. He even invited me to his home. I started to daven, to put on tefillin, things like that.

My parents noticed the change. I can't say they were happy about it either. They were worried that I was in some kind of psychological trouble. I reassured them that everything was okay, and they let me do what I wanted.

But when I told them I wanted to go learn in a yeshivah, they hit the roof. We fought all the time. Rabbi Cohen told my parents that he didn't want to interfere and that at my age they had complete authority over my life. My parents calmed down a lot after he said that. My father was really impressed by Rabbi Cohen. After meeting him he said, "I trust him." On the other hand, he couldn't stand the thought of me becoming *chareidi*.

We finally came to a compromise. I transferred to a religious, but not *frum*, high school. My friends weren't surprised. Some of them had become interested in religion like me, but not to the extent of switching schools.

Over the next couple of months, as I studied in the new high school, I became more and more committed. I reached a point where that school wasn't the right place for me anymore. Again, I found myself facing my parents and asking them to transfer me to a *chareidi* school. My parents listened to what I had to say and didn't argue, but they were opposed to the change.

When my father saw how badly I wanted it, he called a *chareidi* man he knew and asked him to look for a yeshivah for me. The man explained to him that it wasn't so simple, that no *chareidi* yeshivah would agree to accept me. That came as a big surprise. We never thought we'd be refused. We thought they'd welcome us with open arms. Boy, were we wrong.

I talked to the *chareidi* man. He was very nice and explained to me in a nice way that the *chareidi* educational system is very strict and guards against outside influences. He said that this strictness isn't against me personally, but that it's *chareidi* policy and that it's also the reason they're called "*chareidim*," which literally means people who tremble in fear of transgressing any of God's commandments.

I cried and pleaded with him. "Take me to the rabbi of the yeshivah. I'll promise him that I won't bring in any of the outside culture or be a bad influence."

My father got involved. The rejection must have made him realize that these were serious places with a real educational standard. They saw their way as superior, and had no "missionary" interest in getting me to transfer to them.

I met the *rosh yeshivah* of a good *yeshivah ketanah*. He talked with me a little and said he was very impressed, but repeated that he'd have a big problem accepting me because all the boys were *chareidi* boys whose fathers learned in *kollel*. It was a serious *yeshivah ketanah*.

The *chareidi* man who had gotten me the interview used his connections to pressure them into accepting me. He went to Rav Steinman, who today is the *gadol hador*. Rav Steinman thought it wasn't a good idea for me to go straight into a *chareidi* yeshivah, but he agreed to see me first before he arrived at a final decision.

The *chareidi* man took me and my father to Rav Steinman's house in Bnei Brak. It was an amazing experience. His home was straight out of a legend of old. Plain walls, furniture from a hundred years ago. A lot of *chareidim* were waiting there, and then it was our turn.

We went into the room. The *Rav* sat on a bed, in a shirt and hat. Time stood still as he looked at me intently without saying a word.

"*Kevod HaRav,*" the *chareidi* said to him, "this is the boy from the secular home who wants to be *chareidi*. He's learning in a religious high school and now he wants to learn in a *yeshivah ketanah.*"

"Are you learning Gemara?" Rav Steinman asked me.

"Yes."

"Which Gemara?"

I told him.

He asked me a question, and I answered him correctly. Then he asked a *kashe* that I immediately recognized as one Tosafos asks. I gave him the answer that's written on the page.

He asked me if I was satisfied with that answer. I thought a little and then told him that I wasn't, because it didn't fit the facts in the Gemara.

He laughed and said that my answer was a *kashe* in the Rashba, and he went on to tell me the *teirutz*.

Then he asked me, "How will you cope with the *yetzer hara?*"

I thought it over before answering, "I'm already bar mitzvah, so I have a *yetzer hatov.*"

He really enjoyed my answer. He shook my hand and said, "I bless you that you grow in Torah and *yiras Shamayim,* and that you always triumph over your *yetzer hara.*"

The meeting ended. He hadn't said anything about what we'd come to ask.

I was tense for the next day or two, and then I got a positive answer from the yeshivah. Rav Steinman had decided that they could give me a chance.

I don't want to name the yeshivah, but it was one of the best in the country.

My parents made one condition: that I sleep at home.

I bought a hat and a suit. My father paid for everything, but I could see that underneath it all he was very nervous.

I entered *shiur aleph* during summer *zman*, filled with a burning desire to succeed. I learned day and night, davened with total concentration and deep feeling, and was meticulous about doing mitzvos the right way.

Every Shabbos I walked miles from the town where we lived to the yeshivah. It didn't seem like a big deal at the time, because it was something I really wanted to do.

By the end of the *zman*, I was already considered the best boy in the *shiur*.

In *shiur beis*, I was given the best *chavrusos* and fit in like I'd always been part of that world. I picked up all the nuances of the *yeshivah velt*, the talk, the hand gestures during learning. Even the way I looked was perfect, from the angle of my hat to the way my tie was knotted. I have to give credit to a good friend there who helped me get the right hat and not one that needs a blessing of "thanks for making me ears." He kept me from making mistakes like buying white sports socks and stuff like that.

I also made sure to find out about the political infighting in the *chareidi* world, to know who was against who, something the rest of my yeshivah friends had absolutely zero interest in.

From a nonreligious kid who didn't even know how to say Shema Yisrael, I became a real *yeshivah bachur*. You couldn't tell I wasn't brought up that way.

At some point, I began to understand what Rav Steinman meant when he talked about battling the *yetzer hara*. You've gotta understand that in my house, the television was on all day long, including Shabbos and holidays. And I was home.

The whole family would sit and watch some program, and I would learn on the porch. Sometimes I'd hear laughter; sometimes I'd catch snatches of conversation that caught my interest. I'd have to fight with myself not to ask, "Hold it – what happened?"

Every summer, my family traveled abroad. We went all over the world. You can't imagine how hard it was for me to stay stuck in a hotel while the whole family traveled on Shabbos to enjoy all kinds of "once in a lifetime" experiences. I don't think there's another *yeshivah bachur* in the world who's faced these kinds of tests.

But I survived. I gritted my teeth and kept on learning, davening, doing mitzvos, and being the best boy in the yeshivah.

I made it to *shiur gimmel*. My standing in the yeshivah couldn't have been better. Everyone had forgotten that just three or four years earlier, I hadn't been religious at all.

But I didn't forget. I had plenty of reminders every day.

❊　　❊　　❊

Then my sister got married.

It was a fancy wedding, and I had to take a lot of time off from yeshivah for it. For example, they made her a surprise video. Filming it took a lot of time, and, as a family member, I had to be there.

Stuff like this drew me like a magnet, and what all the temptations hadn't managed to do, this dramatic production did.

In the beginning, I stood my ground. I knew the *yetzer hara* was knocking at my door. I tried to fight, but I reached a point where I didn't have the strength to stand firm. I gave in.

It happened fast. I dropped out of yeshivah – without saying good-bye, without anything. They thought I was sick. They called, but I wouldn't take any calls. Finally my mother told them the truth, that I was undergoing a crisis and trying to decide what to do. They didn't bother us anymore. They gave us our space. But they did send me a message that everyone loved me and that they missed me.

I took off the hat and coat, and dropped all Torah and mitzvah observance. I registered at a local public school. I still put on tefillin and tried to keep Shabbos and eat kosher, but I went back to being secular.

Deep down, I feel that I'm still a *yeshivah bachur*, but a *yeshivah bachur* who surrendered to his *yetzer hara*.

The *yetzer hara* is holding me prisoner. Maybe I'll escape. But in the meantime, this is reality. The reason I'm writing this story is to say two things.

One is that I think if my parents had thrown me out of the house, I'd still be a real *yeshivah bachur*, because I wouldn't have the *yetzer hara* and I wouldn't have any conflict. The fact that my parents kept me in the house and treated me so well caused a sort of competition between my home and family and the new path in life I'd chosen – and the house won. As of now.

So this is a message to *chareidi* parents. Don't ever kick out a kid who is going off the *derech*, because then he really won't have any choice. Always keep the love and warmth going, and leave the door open. In the end, that will win out.

I once read a story that gave over this point in a very effective way. It was about an argument between the sun and the wind over which one could get a person to take off his coat. The wind blew, and the man pulled his coat around him more tightly. The sun blazed, and the man couldn't wait to take off his coat. Warmth is always better than cold. In my case, it gave the *yetzer hara* the upper hand.

The second thing I want to say, and this is my main message, is to my friends back in the yeshivah I left: I miss you, and I know that what I did caused a commotion and maybe even a little spiritual cooling off.

I feel bad about that. After all, I was given a chance that no secular kid gets, to enroll in an established *chareidi* yeshivah that even *chareidi* kids have a hard time getting into.

I'm especially ashamed when I think of how I betrayed the trust of Rav Steinman, the *gadol hador*. So I'd like to say a few words of encouragement.

Don't envy me. Would you envy a prisoner?

I'm not a captive like Gilad Shalit. No one is holding me here by force. But I'm a captive of my *yetzer hara*. I miss the yeshivah life, the learning, the atmosphere, the feeling of holiness and purity, and I'm not very happy right now. I don't feel good about myself or my choices. Sometimes things are rough. You have no idea just how rough.

But it's hard for me, hard to escape my captivity. Sometimes I want to go back, but I don't dare because I know I won't last. So meanwhile, I stay in captivity. But you, my friends in yeshivah – don't get turned off. Learn from me how strong the *yetzer hara* is and be happy that you don't have this conflict. Be happy that your parents are glad you're learning and davening and growing stronger in your *yiras Shamayim*.

And daven that I escape my captivity. Until then, writing this story is the only thing I can do from my place of captivity to minimize the damage.

I'm signing this, "From the captive child who escaped to freedom and was recaptured." That says it all.

11

Forgive and Forget?

The story I want to tell happened over twenty-five years ago.

We were students in one of the best seminaries. As happens, various friendships formed among the girls, some close, and some casual.

One friendship stood out in particular, the one between Na'ava and Avital. You couldn't miss it. Some considered it too close; others saw it as the ideal, an amazing bond of sharing and caring. Many girls looked at the friendship with unconcealed jealousy.

One day, Avital came to school all shaken up. She told us she'd gotten an anonymous letter filled death threats. We thought she was joking, but she said she'd prove it by bringing the letter to class the next day.

When we saw the letter, we couldn't believe it. It was a piece of hate mail, something none of us had ever seen before. In it were explicit threats against Avital and her family. Perhaps because it was so well written, it terrified us more than if it had been filled with all kinds of random insults and curses.

As Avital's best friend, Na'ava was very supportive and did her best to calm her down. But this letter was something that would scare even a mature adult, let alone an eighteen-year-old girl.

The next day, Avital came to school agitated. She'd been on the receiving end of some threatening phone calls. Someone with a strange voice had threatened and intimidated not only her, but other members of her family.

She was called into the principal's office, and met with the guidance counselor. The incident became the talk of the seminary.

A week passed, and the harassment continued. Avital became a shadow of her former self. And then, all of a sudden, she stopped talking to Na'ava. No one knew what had happened between them, but the break was so sharp, you couldn't help but notice.

Na'ava tried to talk to her, but Avital just walked away. During one break between classes, everything exploded. Na'ava tried to corner Avital in the school yard, and then everyone, and I mean *everyone*, heard Avital shout or scream, "If you talk to me again, I'll call the police!"

The whole seminary was in an uproar. What else was there to think but that Na'ava was the one who had harassed Avital? But why in the world would Na'ava do something like that? They were best friends!

The next week was a nightmare. Na'ava didn't come to school, and Avital was out a lot too. Rumors flew thick and fast, especially the one about a private investigator being called in. People whispered that Na'ava had taken a lie detector test that showed she was telling the truth...or lying, depending on which version you heard. We talked about nothing else.

After that week, they both returned to seminary, but not to their friendship. Once again, they weren't talking to each other, but this time, the break was total.

This wasn't the only change, though. The shadow of suspicion had fallen heavily on Na'ava and stayed there. All fingers pointed at her, not that anyone said so outright. But no one cleared her name outright either. The girls knew for a fact that she had harassed and threatened her best friend. In retrospect, their friendship had been nothing more than a neurotic obsession that was doomed from the start. Too bad it had to end the way it did.

Socially, it dealt a deathblow to Na'ava. While Avital made friends with other girls and moved on, Na'ava found herself isolated. Not everyone stopped talking with her, but who wanted to be friends with a girl who had sent threatening letters? And what threats!

Na'ava, who'd been a popular girl, always surrounded by a circle of admiring friends, turned into a sad, lonely outsider. Avital would have nothing to do with her, and the rest of the girls kept their distance too.

A year passed, and then another. Avital got engaged first. The whole class came to her wedding – except for Na'ava.

Six months later, Na'ava got engaged. She was worried that only a few girls, if any, would come to dance at her wedding, but I made sure they were there. How? By going from girl to girl and practically forcing each and every one of them to come. I talked to them about a bride's tears, about the grudge she might carry, and, believe it or not, even about the possibility that Na'ava hadn't been the one behind the ugly campaign of harassment.

Not a single one of the girls bought that last argument. "Give me a break," they said to me. "Who else could it have been?"

But they agreed to come because of the other points I mentioned, so at least the wedding was a happy one. The girls danced and rejoiced with Na'ava as if nothing had happened.

Half a year later, I got engaged. Na'ava came to my wedding, though I was certain she knew nothing about what I'd done for her.

Seven children were born to her, one right after the other. I was also blessed with children. We lived at opposite ends of the same neighborhood, so we ran into each other occasionally. Whenever we met, I'd look at her and wonder if she still remembered what had happened in seminary. I had the feeling that under the surface, a storm of suppressed pain and fury still raged. The Na'ava of today bore no resemblance to the carefree girl she'd once been.

But then again, maybe it just seemed that way to me.

Our children grew up, learning in yeshivos and seminaries, and reached the age of marriage. One day, I got a call from Na'ava. She told me they'd offered her son a *shidduch* with a girl in my daughter's class.

I asked for the name of the girl so that I could check her out.

"You probably know her," Na'ava said. "Remember our classmate Rivka? It's her daughter."

"I'll check it out," I said, quickly ending the conversation.

When my husband came home, he found me sitting there numbly, my face as white as chalk.

"What happened?" he asked in alarm.

"They're suggesting Rivka's daughter for Na'ava's son."

"So? What's the problem?"

"I think I have to stop the *shidduch*."

"Because of what happened in sem?"

"Yes," I said. "That's exactly why."

"Don't you think enough time has gone by?"

"Maybe time has gone by, but some things should never happen."

"I still don't see what the problem is," my husband said. "With all due respect, they're not suggesting her son to one of our own daughters. Rivka knows exactly what you know, and if she doesn't think it's a good idea, she can say so and that will be that."

"But that's the problem," I said. "Rivka said they're willing to move forward."

"Good," my husband said. "Even though she knows what she knows, she's decided that childhood arguments bear no relevance now, and she's ready for her daughter to marry Na'ava's son. What right do you have to sabotage this *shidduch*?"

I began to cry bitterly. My husband panicked and didn't know what to do with himself. "What happened?" he asked. "Why are you crying?"

"You don't understand," I said to him between sobs. "I'm not worried about Rivka. I'm worried about Na'ava."

"Na'ava? Why would you be worried about Na'ava? She harassed Avital, yet people are still willing to marry her son. What's the big deal?"

"Na'ava never harassed Avital, and for your information, she underwent a lie detector test that showed she was telling the truth."

"Okay, then what's the problem?"

"The problem is that I know who was behind the harassment. I knew it even then, but I did nothing about it. *It was Rivka.* She admitted it to me, but made me promise not to tell a soul. All these years I've been living with this lie, keeping it buried inside. The only thing I did for Na'ava was to make sure her wedding wasn't spoiled. How can I let her become in-laws with the person who ruined her life? I just can't let it happen."

I spent the night telling my husband everything I knew about what had happened. The seminary had hired a private investigator who found out the truth. He brought proof that the phone calls originated from Rivka's house, and cleared Na'ava's name completely. But because Rivka's parents – who had status in the community – begged him not to reveal this, it didn't become public knowledge. The school administration accepted Rivka's promise never to do anything like that again, and then they notified Na'ava that she could return to school.

"And that's all?" my husband asked.

"Yes, that's all! The whole school suspected an innocent girl! Na'ava lost her best friend and became a social outcast – and not a single person stood up for her. Why should she link her family with that snake? No way!"

My husband was shocked. He didn't know what shocked him more, the fact that his wife had remained silent at an injustice like this all these years, or the fact that his wife was going to ruin a *shidduch*. He wasn't happy with either, but now that I'd told him about it after years of silence and a terrible burden of guilt, I decided to take it to the end.

My husband and I went to our rav. He listened to the story and was appalled. He said he'd never had this kind of question posed to him and wasn't sure how it should be handled. He asked us to wait a day because he wanted to talk it over with a *gadol*.

The next day, he made time in his schedule for us again. He told us that he had received a halachic ruling. Since I'd been asked for information, I *did* need to warn my friend about the *shidduch*. I should tell her that I had information about the mother from the past that would make her want to drop the suggestion. That's all he gave me permission to say.

So that's what I did. I called Na'ava and apologized for taking two days to get back to her, and then I said, "Listen, Na'ava, there's something I need to tell you. I have information about Rivka from the past that might make you want to drop the *shidduch*."

"Information from the past?" Na'ava said. "It can only be one thing."

I didn't say anything.

"She's the one who harassed Avital?"

I didn't reply.

"I suspected as much," she said. "I'm happy that at least now I know."

We talked for hours. Na'ava told me to what extent that event changed her life, how heartbroken she was over it, and how it nearly destroyed her faith in humanity. She harbored a lot of resentment toward the administration for not clearing her name, and toward her parents for not demanding that they do so.

"You see," she said, "some people are just trampled on. No one cares about their feelings or about justice. The polygraph proved I was telling the truth. The administration told us they'd cleared my name of all suspicion and said I could come back. They didn't want to name the person who was really behind the harassment because they wanted the story to end quietly. What they did was to nearly end the story of my life quietly."

Before we hung up, Na'ava thanked me for the information I'd given her and promised not to reveal that I was the one who told her.

Two weeks later, Na'ava called me. "I didn't want you to hear it from someone else. I want to let you know that my son is getting engaged...to Rivka's daughter."

I was speechless.

Na'ava told me that by the time I got back to her, the couple had already met once and both wanted to continue. My call put her in a sticky situation. After thinking it through, she decided to pick up the phone to Rivka and ask for a meeting.

They met without anyone else knowing about it.

"I need to talk to you about something from the past," Na'ava began. "I strongly suspect that you were the one behind the harassment of Avital and her family. Am I right?"

Rivka burst out crying and admitted the truth. She said that her social standing had been low, and she'd been very jealous of the close friendship between Na'ava and Avital. She told Na'ava that she didn't know how she could have done something like that, and said she'd never done anything like it before or since.

She said she was in therapy for a long time after the incident, and was now a different person.

"But what about me?" Na'ava asked plaintively. Without warning, all her pent-up emotions burst out in deep, racking sobs.

"I cried there for half an hour," Na'ava told me. "I didn't need to say a thing because everything was in those tears: the pain, the loneliness, the anger, the injustice. Everything. But in the end, I had a choice. I could continue to stay angry, or I could end it. I was being given a chance to close the circle with the very same person who had hurt me so terribly. It would be a kind of *tikkun*, and, if you will, a victory.

"I called you now to thank you. I don't want you to feel bad about trying to stop the *shidduch*. You did the right thing. You helped me fix something very broken in my life, and for that I'll always be grateful. Don't worry. Rivka will never know you were the one who told me."

The *shidduch* progressed to a happy conclusion. The couple married and established a beautiful home, and the in-laws appeared to get along well too.

As for me, aside from the obvious message that schools may need to pay closer attention to socially weaker students, giving them the protection and backing they lack, I got a major insight into the power to forgive and forget – an ability that helps the forgiver no less than the one forgiven.

12

"It Hurts! Thank You, Hashem!"

If you're looking for a story with a happy ending, you'll have to look elsewhere. My story doesn't have a good beginning or a good middle, and the end is the worst you've ever heard.

But if you're looking for universal meaning, here it is. Just don't say I didn't warn you.

❀　　❀　　❀

I grew up secular. I was a lifeguard. I had no Shabbos, no holidays, no nothing. I had a home in Bat Yam and I was doing okay, but someone who loves money never has enough. I took a course to become a pool manager and got a job doing that. Sometimes I'd see religious people at the pool during the separate hours and I'd feel a pang of jealousy at the way they lived, but I was trapped in my lifestyle.

I decided to go to Miami and make money big time.

I went to become a millionaire and came back a billionaire, because I came back religious. How did it happen? I saw how empty everything was. I went to a Torah class and was mesmerized, even though I'd never been able sit still for long. Believe it or not, I'd always put on tefillin. I used to close the door to the lifeguard's hut and pray.

A year after I became religious, my wife got diabetes and with it a whole host of medical issues cropped up. She underwent bypass surgery, but her health deteriorated to the point where she had to be in a wheelchair.

We were left with no health and no wealth. We came back to Israel and things got worse. We sold our apartment and became destitute.

❀   ❀   ❀

During this period, I saw an ad saying that the Shavei Shomron settlement was looking for a lifeguard. I was chosen out of fifty applicants, and I began to work there.

And that was exactly when...the intifada started. We coped with rock throwing and shooting, daily occurrences.

Along with my work at the pool, I was also a driver. Like everyone else, I had the car maintenance and repairs taken care of by the Arabs in a nearby village. One day, I drove to the garage of the Arab mechanic who used to repair my car, and saw three taxis ahead of me.

"There's a problem with the fuses," the mechanic said. "Let me take care of it for you."

In the meantime, I went to buy vegetables. I bought a few shekels worth and gave the owner a one-hundred-shekel bill. He went to get change from somewhere, and in the meantime, another guy walked into the store. I don't know why, but I suspected him of being a terrorist. He looked at me, I looked at him, and I started talking. He didn't look very friendly, to put it mildly, but I had an Uzi submachine gun and, you know, looks can't kill but an Uzi certainly can. Then he left.

The minute he left, I ran for my car. He was waiting there for me with a friend. The problem was that his friend was carrying an M16 rifle. Just like that, he pointed it at me and started to shoot from a distance of about fifteen feet. I bent over and ran to the other side of the car. I crawled inside it as the bullets flew past my head. I saw the shots hit the doors and slam into the dashboard, missing me one after the other.

I wasn't afraid. I'd fought on the Hermon in the Yom Kippur War, so fear was not part of my arsenal. I always felt Hashem was with me.

There was no break in the shooting. With my weapon drawn, I flung open the other door. I aimed the Uzi at them, and they got scared and ran away.

Instead of fleeing, I got out of the car and chased after them. I released the safety catch, aimed, and pulled the trigger. The weapon made no sound. I whipped out a cartridge from my pocket as I ran, and tried again. Nothing. The Uzi didn't fire. And then I felt that I'd been wounded. One of the bullets must have hit me. I was losing blood, but I kept on chasing them toward an olive grove. A woman shouted for people to come help them.

If they'd had any sense, they would have realized that my gun wasn't working and they'd have shot me. But all they thought about was that I was running after them with a weapon. They were sure that if I closed the gap, I'd shoot them.

When they went into the grove, my good judgment kicked in, and I realized it was time for me to turn back. I went back up to the road to find half the village waiting for me. I pointed my weapon at them, they all lay down on the ground in fear, and I started to run out of the village, every once in a while turning around with the Uzi, which wasn't worth more than a broomstick.

There wasn't a single Israeli vehicle on the road, and taxis whizzed past my weapon. Suddenly I saw a car with an Arab driver trying to make a U-turn. I went over to him with my Uzi aimed, opened the door on the passenger side, and said to him, "Sit here." He moved over.

"Now go back to the driver's seat," He moved back, and I get in the car, all the while keeping his head in the sights.

"Have mercy on me!" he shouted. "I have a wife and children!"

"Just drive to the main road, and nothing will happen to you."

He flew out of there, and it wasn't long before we reached the entrance to Shavei Shomron.

I was afraid the settlement's security guards would shoot at the car, thinking it belonged to a terrorist. I leaned halfway out the window and shouted, "Don't shoot!" The guard recognized me and lowered his weapon. The car stopped. I got out and said to the driver, "Get out of here." He flew out of there faster than the speed of light.

"Hey!" the guard said. "You're full of blood. Lay down here." He forced me to lie down. I didn't want to. I opened up the gun and a bullet suddenly flew out, nearly hitting the guard. Pandemonium broke out.

That's when I realized that I was wounded, bleeding, and in pain. A lot of pain.

Ever since I'd become religious, I'd gotten used to saying, "It hurts! Thank You, Hashem! Thank You, Hashem. It hurts." The guard was sure I'd taken a bullet to my head, not my chest.

My wife arrived in her wheelchair. I kept screaming, "It hurts! Thank You, Hashem!" until an ambulance came to take me to the hospital. Another minute, and I would have arrived at the world of truth instead because of all the blood I'd lost.

I was there in the hospital for nine days. The Shin Bet (Israel Security Agency) came to interrogate me. I asked to be released.

"It's a bullet wound," the doctor said. "You're not going anywhere."

"Oh yes I am," I told him. I pulled out the IV and got dressed to go home.

"If you insist on leaving, sign here first."

That's exactly what I did.

A few years went by. We had to leave Shavei Shomron because my wife's health deteriorated. We moved to Elad.

One day, my wife said to me, "For fifteen years you've been caring for me as I sit in this wheelchair, helping me with everything, giving me the best of care. I'm going to put in a good word for you upstairs."

"Why are you talking like that?" I said to her. "How about putting in a good word for me here on earth? That's good enough for me."

"Can I ask you to do something?"

"Till half the kingdom, but not my crown," I joked.

She got a little irritated at that.

"Okay," I said to her. "I'm your slave. Does that sound any better?"

She laughed and said, "Okay, put the crown back on fast." Then she added, "I want you to promise me that when I die, you'll get married again."

"Don't talk like that. When you reach a hundred, I'll push you in a wheelchair made by Mercedes."

She wanted me to promise, but I refused.

That night, my wife died. She was such a special person, so kind and good, always praying and doing mitzvos and good deeds. I'm sure she went straight up to Gan Eden.

❈　　❈　　❈

I mourned her for two years and couldn't bring myself to do what she'd asked. Then someone suggested a woman whose soul was a twin of my first wife's. She was kind and good, special, always doing mitzvos and good deeds.

I felt as though my wife had sent her to me so that I'd be happy after all those hard years.

The wedding took place in Ramat Gan in the *kollel* of Rabbi David Levy, who's called "Dede."

Dede deserves a story of his own. He was stricken with polio as a child, and it left him paralyzed. He became religious in his teens. His wife Rivka, was, like him, a wheelchair user and a returnee to Judaism.

Dede and his wife were known as extraordinarily warm and caring people. On Shabbos, they had an open house, where everyone was treated to a meal fit for a king and felt like family. They also worked in kiruv sponsored by the Wolfson Foundation, which is how Rivka came to know my second wife, Yehudit, and that's how they came to be involved in our *shidduch* and wedding, which took place in Dede's *kollel*.

I became attached to Dede heart and soul after the wedding, and since my wife was his wife's best friend, we became very close friends and spent time at each other's homes.

Five months ago, we vacationed together in Tiberias. Dede was driving his specially equipped car that had two steering wheels. He'd wheel his wheelchair into the car, lock it in place, and be all set to go. Despite his disability, he got to places faster than most people. Instead of needing other people's help, he'd be there first to help them.

It was a fabulous vacation. One day, a little after noon, Dede called me. "Want to join us?" he asked. "We're going to the Tal Forest."

"You go on ahead. I'll follow you in my car."

"We'll go together," Dede insisted.

My wife took a bag with some mangoes and sat next to Rivka, who was in her wheelchair. I got in next to Dede, who drove. Their children sat in the back seat.

We set out for our destination. On the way, my wife suggested that I let Dede taste the mangoes.

"He's driving," I told her. "He won't be able to eat any mangoes until we get there."

We reached Migdal Junction. As I told you, Dede's car had two steering wheels, one regular, and the second, smaller and set lower down. At the Migdal Junction, the road curves to the left at an almost ninety-degree angle. Dede turned the wheel to take the curve, and then tried to turn it to the right, to follow the road, but the wheel didn't move. Dede pulled harder. Suddenly I saw a truck heading straight at us. I looked at Dede, who was sweating bullets, and then back at the truck. Dede was still trying to pull the car to the right, but the steering wheel was frozen.

For some reason, the truck driver stepped on the gas instead of slowing down. Maybe he thought that if he drove fast enough he'd miss us.

I reached over and pulled hard on the steering wheel, but it was locked. Then came the crash.

I felt the truck slam into us. I might have lost consciousness for a few seconds. The minute I came to, lying there in the wreck, I was hit by excruciating pain. But I was alive, and, as usual, I shouted, "Thank You very much, Hashem! It hurts, thank You, thank You. It hurts!"

The car was totaled. I saw people crowding around, breaking open my door, holding me. I felt like they were tearing me apart. "It hurts, but thank You. It's all from You."

They got me out, writhing in pain, and lay me down on the ground. I stared up into the sky, waiting for them to bring out my wife. I saw them break open the middle door and pull out Rivka, Dede's wife. She was in shock, but she was alive. They put her down next to me.

Then suddenly I saw them taking out from the middle a high stretcher. On it was a person who was covered. I realized that it was my beloved wife.

"Take off the blanket!" I shouted. "You're smothering her." People tried to get me to calm down. "It's okay," they murmured. That's when I realized that this "okay" was the most not okay thing you could imagine.

The ambulance arrived and took me to Poriya Hospital in Tiberias. There they gave me shots of morphine to dull the excruciating pain, but it didn't work.

"It hurts! Thank You, Hashem," I cried out.

They brought me to the ICU, on the way telling me that Dede had been killed instantly.

I saw Dede's son and daughter nearby, both of them wounded and in shock.

"How is my wife, Yehudit?" I asked them.

They didn't answer, though they knew.

I had broken ribs, a dislocated shoulder, and a spleen torn to shreds. I was bleeding internally and in constant pain – but more than anything, I was terrified because part of me knew my wife's fate.

✳   ✳   ✳

A few hours passed. A police officer came over to me and said, "Can I ask you if you know what happened to your wife, Yehudit?"

When he said that, I knew right away. "She's dead?"

"Yes."

I felt like my world was destroyed.

Job, who went through so many trials and tribulations, said, "Why, God?" And God answered him, "I created the world and don't ask questions." I felt like Job. I didn't ask any questions, but I felt like my whole world was destroyed around me.

In the morning, they moved me to a ward. Two good friends, Rabbi Bognim and Rabbi Porush, were waiting there for me. Can you imagine? They'd waited for me all night. What wonderful people.

"Reuven," they asked me, "do you want to be transferred to a hospital in the center of the county?"

"Yes."

It was Friday. They put me in an ambulance. We drove with the siren blaring, and within thirty-five minutes we arrived at Tel Hashomer.

I had blood clots that were moving toward my heart. All it would have taken was one to kill me if they hadn't caught it in time. We got to the trauma center, and eventually they operated and took out my spleen.

❋   ❋   ❋

That's the story. I lost two wonderful wives, special, righteous women, and I still thank the Creator of the world for giving them to me.

My wife appeared to me in a dream. She said, "Why are you crying? I'm in the world of truth and you're in the world of falsehood. I'll pray for you that you sit with me." That lifted my spirits. I decided that I'd dedicate myself to learning Torah and to my precious children. I'd sit and learn, and Hashem would help me.

I want to thank the thousands of people who prayed for my recovery. The moral of my story is this: If, after all I've been through, I can thank Hashem not only now but all during the pain and tragedy, then every single person who has a healthy spouse, children, and an income – no matter how minimal – has to thank Hashem for each and every minute.

When I lay there bleeding at the entrance to Shavei Shomron and I cried out, "It hurts! Thank You, Hashem!" and then years later at Migdal Junction, my whole body screaming in pain knowing that my beloved, righteous wife was no longer among the living and I shouted, "It hurts! Thank You, Hashem!" it wasn't some conclusion I'd reached, but was coming from a deep place.

I wish everyone a life free of pain, especially pain such as I experienced. The moral of my story? Grab hold of your life with both hands and don't let go. Most of all, thank Hashem for it, because it's good and this world is a place of His loving- kindness. And should you encounter a small pain, always remember my cry: "It hurts! Thank You, Hashem!"

Author's note: I would like to express my deep appreciation to Reb Reuven Goren of Elad for sharing with me his personal story and agreeing to have it published. May it be an elevation for the soul for Rabbi David "Dede" Levy, *z"l*, and for Mrs. Yehudit Goren, *a"h*, and may their souls be bound in the bond of everlasting life.

13

Every Man His Hour

I've carried my story in my heart for many years, and now, even as I tell it to you, it's with a heavy heart.

The reason for the difficulty is that the story is about my brother, my own flesh and blood, but it's about things that every family would prefer to forget. Still, despite the difficulty, I thought it only right to tell the story because of its message.

A lot of time has passed since this story took place, and I've changed certain identifying details. Both factors make it easier for me share it, in the hope it will benefit others.

❁   ❁   ❁

I grew up in a large, prestigious family. We have many *rabbanim* and Torah scholars among us. The entire extended family, beginning with my father and his brothers, each of whom has a large family of over ten children, numbers some one thousand souls, *bli ayin hara*.

Our family also had a double-digit number of children, and we were raised in an atmosphere of spiritual purity. We had no contact with the outside world. Even newspapers didn't enter our home. We were raised to devote ourselves to Torah, prayer, and fear of Heaven, and the results spoke for themselves.

By the way, till this very day I'm convinced that the best way to raise children is behind a protective wall that safeguards them from the worthless pursuits of this world. I know some people scorn this approach, claiming that the more you restrict children, the more they want to break the boundaries. To that I say, not true. The more you restrict them, the *less* they'll want to break the boundaries. Yes, there can always be one out of ten who might leave the path, but that doesn't make our lifestyle bad. In fact, the truth is quite the opposite.

As I'm telling you these things, all the memories come rushing back.

I remember how it started. I was older than my brother by a few years. He was a kid who made trouble in school, got sent home a lot, fought with other boys, and blamed everyone else. My parents treated him gently. They tried to overlook his problems and see him only in a positive light.

I remember the first time we realized that he wasn't just a mischievous kid. It was when the boys in his class starting missing things, like money and small items. Everyone was talking about it, until one day, they caught the culprit in the act.

It was my brother.

He never set foot in our school again. For a family like ours, it wasn't hard to find a different school that very same day – which makes you think about all those families where if a kid makes one mistake, tragically, all doors are closed to him.

He didn't last long at the second school, though – not more than a few months. He used to run away from school. He became friends with problematic kids, swiped candy and trinkets from kiosks, and tormented animals.

No one knew what his story was. He wasn't suffering at home. No one hurt him. He wasn't under any pressure. If anything, he was surrounded by a forgiving atmosphere. But inside of him he had some kind of destructive force that operated full blast.

In eighth grade, he disappeared for a few days. My parents, despite their embarrassment, had no choice but to call the police. The police search found him sleeping on a beach.

Even then, one of the policemen said to my father, "Listen, mister, I don't want to say anything, but from what I know about kids, this kid is headed straight for a life of crime."

At first, my father dismissed it out of hand. But when run-ins with the police became more frequent, my father brought in a *frum* educational expert. The man started working with my brother, but soon gave up. He said that the boy was smart as a whip and quite possibly gifted. But the minute he got an impulse – of whatever kind – he had no tools to stop it.

When my brother entered the teenage years, things got worse. He crossed all red lines. He was violent, he stole, he fought, and he hung around with the worst kind of people. Plenty of attempts were made to rehabilitate him. I remember a period when he went back to wearing a hat and coat, and even returned to yeshivah. It would last two or three months, and then suddenly, out of the blue, he'd do something outrageous and be back on the street.

Once, he lasted six months in yeshivah. Then one fine day, or to be more exact, one fine night, he stole the money and valuables of everyone in the yeshivah and disappeared for a month.

This time they found him on a beach in the south of the country. His hair was down to his shoulders, he'd thrown off his *kippah*, and you couldn't have guessed in a million years that he had any connection to an illustrious *frum* family.

If you knew my father, you'd find it even harder to believe how this precious tzaddik, so pure and holy, found the strength to journey to those dark places with him, all the time trying to understand to what depths his own son had fallen, and yet, through it all, to still treat him with love.

During this time, the educational expert explained to my parents that my brother had a criminal mind and an antisocial personality disorder. He put it bluntly: chances were my brother would spend the rest of his life on the wrong side of the law.

❁ ❁ ❁

I remember those days because by then I was married and my parents asked for my help in going to *rabbanim* for advice. I got a crash course in the workings of the criminal mind and personality disorders. For the first time in my life, I found out that there is such a thing as a person whose illness has no cure. No psychological treatment, no psychiatric medications, not hospitalization, and not even jail would help my brother. It was hard for me to accept that there could exist a person who couldn't change. Such people can't keep a job and can't get married – or, if they do, they can't stay married. They sever ties with their family, repeatedly get entangled with the law, blame everyone in the world but themselves, and do everything in their power to get what they want, without any pangs of conscience or inner moral compass.

They may possess exceptional charisma. They know how to dress well, to make a good impression, to appear sensitive and caring, to get people to like them. But all this is used to attain their goal, which is never a positive one. The minute they achieve what they set out to, it's over. They're gone, leaving in their wake a trail of disappointed, wounded, and hurt people.

I remember the exact moment when I had to tell my parents that their son had no hope of ever changing. I don't wish on anyone having to see the torment on his parents' faces when they're forced to accept, though never fully, that there is nothing they can do to help their child.

Let me take this opportunity to tell readers what an anti-social personality disorder is. It affects some 3 percent of men and 1 percent of women. Here's a short list of the symptoms:

1. Deceitfulness, repeated lying, conning others for personal profit or pleasure
2. Irritability, having a "short fuse," aggressiveness
3. Repeated physical fights or assaults
4. Reckless disregard for the person's safety or that of others
5. Consistent irresponsibility
6. Lack of remorse
7. Frequent actions that warrant imprisonment

I thought facing a loved one's death was the ultimate challenge. But that's exactly how my family and I felt when we were forced to face the fact that we had a brother who was a criminal.

Next came ten years of unbelievable shame and disgrace, run-ins with the law, and even jail terms. Though my brother cut himself off from the family, everyone knew the truth about him, and we had to live with the shame and cope with it. My brothers' and sisters' *shidduchim* suffered from it, but it didn't ruin their chances completely. Everyone understood that he was one in a thousand. One person out of such a large family of God-fearing Torah scholars and tzaddikim was obviously an exception to the rule. Still, it didn't add any points to the *shidduch* résumé.

One day, my brother disappeared. And when I say disappeared, I mean *disappeared*.

My father tried to find out what had happened to him, but it was as if the ground had opened up and swallowed him.

A few months went by, and then my father turned to the police. They didn't know quite what to tell him. "He's almost thirty," they said. "He's a big boy already. He's got every right to disappear if that's what he wants to do."

"Maybe he needs help," my father said. "Maybe he's the victim of a crime."

The police didn't seem worried about such a possibility.

Ten years passed without us hearing anything from him or about him. Meanwhile, my parents married off all their children, and the family grew by leaps and bounds, with grandchildren and even great-grandchildren. My parents felt deep happiness and joy at the beautiful family with which they'd been blessed. I wish it on everyone. But people who really knew them knew that deep down, they ached over this son who had caused them so much anguish and heartbreak, and had then suddenly disappeared.

And then, one day, my parents were called to a meeting. The meeting was to take place in Tel Aviv. The caller told them it was top secret and connected with them. He said they shouldn't worry, but they should make sure to get there within the next few hours.

A few people in civilian clothes were waiting for them when they arrived and informed them that their son had died in the security services. They didn't go into detail, but emphasized that my brother had served the state in recent years by performing various secret, extremely dangerous missions, and that he met his death in an enemy country with which Israel had no diplomatic relations.

My parents were warned not to publicize the matter and were given a reasonable cover story. They were informed that they were entitled to a survivor's pension. They were also told that their son had died a hero's death and that he had played a role in saving the lives of every single citizen of Israel.

A small funeral took place, attended by only the immediate family. He was buried childless and forsaken. We didn't ask too many questions. All we were told was that he had been in the army and had died there. Nothing appeared in the media.

My parents insisted on knowing details, but they didn't get what they asked for. A senior officer met with them and told them that the murky world of the secret service (probably the Mossad or the Shin Bet) sometimes needed exactly those people who had no place in normal society.

"In certain places," he told them, "the state needs people who have a criminal mind. It needs people who can lie, deceive, and do so without any conscience or feelings of regret. We're dealing with animals, and sometimes we need to enlist people who act like animals."

That's what he said, plain and simple.

He said he'd given my brother a choice of spending years behind bars or serving his country, and my brother had chosen to serve his country.

"We don't think he did it for ideological reasons. He didn't think along those lines. But he did good work, maybe even the best work any agent has done in the last few decades. It's not easy to handle people like that," the man told my parents. "You're always afraid that they'll switch sides and sell out for a pot of lentils. But there's no choice. You need them. Normative people don't do the things he was willing to do. I'll say this: he was faithful to the end and did a great service to his people."

In a modest ceremony, my parents received the highest military decoration awarded by the state, conferred on my brother posthumously. My father thought long and hard about going to receive the medal, which was about as valuable as a garlic peel to him, but an inner voice urged him to go anyway, to feel that in the end his son did something useful for our people, if not during his early life, at least before his death. Based on the importance of the award, my brother obviously saved more than a few lives. The fact that to this very day his name and photo have not been published, and we have no idea in which country he operated all those years, indicates that most likely we're talking about matters concerning the fate of the country.

❊   ❊   ❊

The only reason I permit myself to write the story at all is because so many years have passed since it happened. And because of its powerful message that no man is without worth and purpose.

The *Midrash Shocher Tov* brings this thought. King David said to Hashem, "Master of the World, everything You made in Your world is exceptionally beautiful, except for insanity. What purpose is there in insanity? A man goes to the marketplace and rips his clothes and children make fun of him and chase after him, and the whole world laughs at him. Does this give You pleasure?"

Hashem said to David, "David, you find it hard to understand insanity? By your life, you'll need it."

And so it was. When David reached Gat, they went to Avimelech, who was called Achish, their king, and said to him, "Let us kill David, who killed our brother Goliath."

When David saw the great danger awaiting him, especially since he still had Goliath's sword in his possession, he decided to feign insanity to escape. He wrote on the doors, "Achish, king of Gat, owes me a hundred myriads, and his wife, fifty." He drooled, the spittle ran down his beard, and he acted like a fool.

Achish said to them, "Do I lack for madmen that you had to bring this one to me?" and had him sent away.

At that moment, David felt incredibly happy that such a thing as insanity existed in the world, and he composed *Tehillim* 34, which begins, "By David, when he acted insane in the presence of Avimelech, who drove him away, and he left. I will bless Hashem every moment..."

Many wonder why Hashem created people who seem to bring bad to the world. The question becomes urgent when it's personal. That's when a person raises his eyes to the Creator and asks, "Why? To what purpose?"

The story I just shared is yet another proof that every creature created by the Holy One, blessed is He, has a purpose, for good or for bad – and for everything between.

14

Bilke

When you say "Bilke," what comes to most people's minds are *bilkele*, those small rolls we eat at *simchas*. However, to some people, admittedly only a few, the word *Bilke* brings back painful memories of a town in what is now Ukraine, near the borders of Slovakia, Hungary, and Romania, where a flourishing Jewish community existed until the Nazis shipped all of its inhabitants to Auschwitz and murdered them down to almost the very last one.

I'm going to tell you the saddest story you've ever heard, with small glimmers of consolation sprinkled on top, much like a *bilkele* sprinkled with sesame seeds – but only a very few. Don't worry. You're not going to hear the usual story about masses of Jews who lived and in the end died. No, what I'm going to do is put under the magnifying glass one man in particular in a small, forgotten village. His name is Reb Shlomo Gedalowitz.

Bilke has existed for more than six hundred years, ever since 1368. Jews began settling there some three hundred years ago, after the Chmielnicki massacres of Tach V'Tat in 1648–49. Prior to World War II, the town's population stood at 10,000, including three hundred Jewish families. With their large families of, on average, ten to twelve souls, they made up close to a third of the population.

Aside from the rabbis and Torah scholars, the Jews of Bilke earned their living as farmers, forest managers, and distillery owners. Others were wealthy mill owners, bankers, prosperous owners of land and vineyards, as well as cobblers, carpenters, storekeepers, cattle dealers, butchers – and, of course, rebbes and teachers in the local public school.

All the Jewish residents of the village were Torah- and mitzvah-observant. All without exception went to ask the rabbi and *posek* their questions on kashrus.

The rabbis of the community over the generations were well-known men of stature like Rabbi Yaakov Kappel Klein; Rabbi Meir Ezriel, who made aliya in 1909 and became a member of the Eida Hachareidis in Yerushalayim; Rabbi Aharon Mordechai Lieberman; and the last *Rav* of Bilke, Rabbi Naftali Zvi Weiss, son of the famous Grand Rabbi of Spinke, a renowned Chassidic dynasty, who served as *Rav* between 1928 and 1944 – the year the Jews of Bilke were transported to their deaths along with their *Rav*.

Between World War I and World War II, Bilke was under Czechoslovakian rule. The Czechs were benevolent toward the Jews, which caused new winds to blow that threatened the religious life of Bilke. The *Rav* of the city, Rabbi Weiss, led an uncompromising battle against those winds and succeeded to a large extent in strengthening the protective walls guarding religious belief and observance.

A man lived in Bilke, and his name was Shlomo Gedalowitz. Reb Shlomo's father, Rabbi Gedalya, was the one who built Bilke's shul, *mikveh*, and guesthouse. His son, Reb Shlomo, who was born in 1897, was orphaned of his mother at a young age.

Despite this difficult beginning, Shlomo became one of the most prominent personalities in Bilke. Aside from his multifaceted business dealings, he was known as an honest, trustworthy man. He was the one with whom both Jew and gentile could leave their money and goods without fear of him cheating them out of even a single cent.

In 1925, Shlomo married, and little by little became the *rav's* right-hand man.

The Jews of Bilke, who saw Reb Shlomo as a bulwark of strength and discretion, would share their troubles with him. When necessary, he would organize a fund-raising campaign to help discreetly those in need. It was common knowledge that there was one address for any and all problems that cropped up: Reb Shlomo Gedalowitz.

The custom in Bilke was that before Yom Kippur, the *gabbai* of the shul would spread straw on the shul floor so that anyone who wanted to spend the holy night in shul would have a place to rest his head. Reb Shlomo was among those who spent the entire night and day of Yom Kippur in the shul. After Neilah, when the fast was over, Reb Shlomo looked like an angel who needed neither food nor sleep.

That's how it was in Bilke, a small town of Torah and fear of Heaven, good deeds and innocence. And that's how Reb Shlomo was: first and foremost in charity, good deeds, and everything holy.

And so flowed Jewish life in Bilke every day of the year, with tradition and its Jewish character maintained without compromise.

Weddings and other celebrations were a daily occurrence, drawing both those invited...and those not. At every one, Reb Moshe ben Zions, musician and *badchan*, set the tone. The whole town used to come on Shabbos to bless the *chasan*, listen to his speech – and interrupt it. Even the pranks were rich with Jewish tradition, such as on Simchas Torah when they'd tie up the chazzan's legs with the *avnet*, the narrow piece of cloth wrapped around the Torah scroll. In our world, this type of humor looks decidedly unfunny, but in the innocent atmosphere of Bilke, such things brought a smile to everyone's face and created a rare camaraderie.

And the non-Jews? As in all of Europe, externally they maintained cordial relations with their Jewish neighbors. This was a necessity, for the Jews of Bilke, like their fellow Jews throughout Europe, were at the center of all commerce, a fact that made the non-Jews highly dependent on them and filled their hearts with burning jealousy. The time would come when it would be clear to all just how dangerous was this concealed animosity simmering below the surface, hidden behind a smile. Eventually, the pressure cooker of hatred and rage exploded.

Signs of the gentiles' hatred could be seen in an event that took place in 1932 on Pesach. Because that year the last day of the Jewish holiday coincided with Easter, the Jews of Bilke kept everything especially low-key so as not to attract unwanted attention.

The Christians of Bilke had a legend that their church bells didn't ring on Easter because the bells traveled to Rome and rang there. No one knew how, exactly, the bells made the journey, whether they walked or hired a wagon and rode. One thing was certain, though. The bells remained in the steeple, yet they traveled to Rome – and would return in a few days.

That year, though, in the middle of Pesach, the church bells started ringing.

All the Christian residents of the town ran to the church. "How can the bells be ringing? Aren't they in Rome?"

As they stared in wonder, the bells clanged and rang out wildly. Someone mad must have been pulling the bell ropes to make such a racket.

Thousands of Christians ran to see. Thousands of Christians… and one Jew: Reb Shlomo Gedalowitz.

Smart man that he was, he knew that bells don't ring on their own. And he had a good idea who was pulling the ropes.

It was, as he suspected, Yitzchak Friedman, the town's meshuggener. The crowd stormed the bell tower, grabbed Yitzchak, and dragged him outside, ready to lynch him. At that moment, he cried out, "I am a Jew! And the bells didn't travel to Rome!"

The enraged mob began beating him, but he just kept repeating, "I'm a Jew, don't you see? Ha, ha, ha – the bells are here, not in Rome."

He stopped only because he lost consciousness, but that didn't stop the crowd, who continued beating him. He'd have had no chance of surviving if not for a Jew of venerable countenance who endangered his life by running into the raging mob shouting, "Leave him be! Don't you see this is Yitzchak, the crazy one?"

Not that the goyim really cared about Yitzchak's profession or the status of his health. The vast quantities of hatred bottled up inside them demanded release, and when they saw Reb Shlomo Gedalowitz, they fell upon him as well.

But Reb Shlomo locked eyes with several of them whose money and goods he was holding. They got the message: if Reb Shlomo went, their money would go with him. They shielded the pair with their bodies and dragged him, along with the unconscious Yitzchak, to the Jewish street.

❀   ❀   ❀

Yitzchak the meshuggener had not yet recovered from his wounds when another blow fell on Bilke, and I'm not talking about World War II.

Reb Isaac Hersh Teichman was Bilke's milkman. He was a simple, God-fearing Jew, scrupulous in his observance.

Isaac Hersh's wife was called "Putter Yidene," or "Butter Jewess," because she sold butter. Her customers ranged from the gentiles of the town to the illustrious Doft family, whose head was the posek of the town, who were known to eat only *chalav Yisrael*.

The Teichmans had only one child, Miriam. She sometimes accompanied her mother to deliver the dairy products. When she got older, her mother sent her alone.

Reb Isaac Hersh and his wife had no idea that their only daughter was mingling with the gentiles until the sorry day when she told them that she had decided to marry one of the non-Jewish farm boys.

In Bilke, where Jews had lived for hundreds of years without even a single incident of intermarriage or apostasy, the milkman and his wife were shocked beyond belief. At first, they sat as if made of stone. Then they tried to convince her to give up her foolish idea. Finally, they cried and pleaded with her to spare them the shame and anguish. When they saw she couldn't be swayed, they decided to turn to the only person who could be entrusted with such a matter: Reb Shlomo Gedalowitz.

Reb Shlomo took them straight to Rav Naftali Zvi Weiss.

This was the first time such a question had been presented to the *Rav* of Bilke. After listening intently, he told them, "Bring the girl to me. I want to speak with her."

Miriam tried everything to get out of speaking with the *rav*. In the end, though, she acquiesced to her parents' pleas, and agreed to go see him.

The *rav* sat smoking his pipe. "Your father told me," he said to her. "I don't need to explain to you what a terrible thing this is.

Have you thought deeply about your decision? Did you consider what such a thing would do to your parents, the community, the Jewish people? The Torah in *Devarim*, chapter seven, verse three, says, 'You shall not intermarry with them. You shall not give your daughter to his son, and you shall not take his daughter for your son.' How will you live with your conscience? How will you be able to look your parents and the rest of the Jews in the eye? God forbid you should do such a thing!"

Miriam was silent for a while, and then said these exact words. "Rabbi, it's fate. The die is cast. I don't have the strength to change it. I already promised to marry him, and I can't go back on my word. Sorry, but two days from now I will convert, and in another week, I'll marry him."

Four people stared at her in trepidation: the *rav*, her parents, and Reb Shlomo Gedalowitz.

"I see that despite your having already decided," Reb Shlomo said to her, "you're doing this reluctantly and not out of *chutzpah* and a desire to cause pain."

"That's true," the girl said. "I love my parents and I love Judaism, but the die is cast, and I can't overcome my desire to marry him."

"If you love your religion, why don't you stay Jewish?" Reb Shlomo asked her.

"Is such a thing possible?" the girl asked.

"According to the law, it's possible," Reb Shlomo said. "Ask the goy to give in to you the way you're giving in to him."

Miriam thought for a moment and then addressed the *rav* respectfully. "I'm so touched by what was just suggested that I promise I will never, ever forsake my religion. I'll stay Jewish, as will my children."

Several days later, Miriam left her parents' house and married the Christian fellow, marking the first intermarriage in Bilke's history.

Naturally, her parents did not attend the wedding, nor did any other Jew in Bilke. The gentiles celebrated in style, happy at having ensnared a Jewish soul, a possibility that had never before occurred to them. Miriam's parents mourned their daughter. As far as they were concerned, their Miriam no longer existed.

❁   ❁   ❁

And then the year 5698/1938 arrived. The *Rav* of Bilke asked that the Hebrew letters signifying the year – *taf, reish, tzaddi, ches* – be transposed so as not to spell out the word for murder. The republic of Czechoslovakia ceased to exist because the murderous villain Hitler, may his name be blotted out, demanded the Sudetenland for Germany. Bilke now became part of Hungary, and the life of the Jews changed immediately.

The Hungarians began by enforcing restrictions closely modeled after the infamous Nuremberg laws. Jewish stores were boycotted; Jews were restricted to living in certain designated areas; they were subjected to a curfew; they were forbidden to practice medicine, law, and dentistry; and they had to wear the yellow star.

In Av 5701/August 1941, the Hungarians rounded up tens of thousands of Jews who could not prove their Hungarian citizenship despite having lived in the country for generations. About one hundred of them were residents of Bilke. They were told they were being expelled to the country where they or their ancestors were born.

Among the one hundred were Reb Shlomo Gedalowitz, his wife, and their two children. They had no time for good-byes. Within twenty-five minutes, they were shoved into cattle cars and transported from the town where they and their ancestors were born and raised.

Bilke was shrouded in sadness. One hundred of its people, flesh of their flesh, had been torn away – and all because they couldn't produce the documents demanded. The discovery that Reb Shlomo Gedalowitz and his family were among the deported made things much worse, because he was the glue that held them all together.

Despite the pain, they held out hope that when it was all over, hopefully in a few months' time, they'd return to Bilke.

What none of them could know was that all the thousands of Hungarians who couldn't prove their identity were shipped to the Ukrainian forests near Kamenitz, where the German, Hungarian, and Ukrainian killers machine-gunned them down and buried them in a mass grave.

Of the one hundred people taken from Bilke, only one returned. Miraculously, this single survivor of that massacre returned to Bilke to tell what had happened to the others.

That one person was none other than Reb Shlomo Gedalowitz. His wife and two children perished in the Ukrainian killing field and were buried in a mass grave. He returned because he had nowhere else to go, and because he wanted to warn the residents of Bilke and shake them out of their complacency.

The fear and panic that gripped the town's residents served its purpose. Now they knew who and what they were dealing with, and the last traces of their naiveté vanished.

Despite his personal tragedy, Reb Shlomo, though sad and broken-hearted, continued to help lead the shattered community. The Jews were now at the mercy of the anti-Semitic Hungarian nationalists and locals, who shed their masks of congeniality and took over Jewish stores and businesses. They did everything to humiliate, debase, and exploit the Jews – as well as take their lives.

The next two years found the Jews of Bilke in a fight for survival. Frightening reports reached them, but hope beat in their hearts that the ugly events would not reach Hungary. There were prayers of "I lift my eyes to the mountains; from where will my help come?" to "How much longer can this go on?" The Jews of Bilke, like all of Hungarian Jewry, sat and waited, never dreaming that the fate of Polish Jewry was moving on a conveyor belt directly to them.

In 5704/1944, after Pesach, right before the end of the war, a notice of expulsion was issued to the Jews of Hungary. They were gathered in the ghetto until Shavuos. During the three days preceding the festival, the Jews of Bilke, along with their fellow Jews from nearby towns and villages, were loaded into freight cars, about one hundred to a car, and sent to Auschwitz.

That's how the entire community of Bilke was brought to the altar of sacrifice, from youth to the elderly; men, women, and children, including: the rav of the community, Rav Naftali Zvi Weiss; the ritual slaughterer, Rabbi Yehoshua Doft; the head of the community, Rabbi Chaim Isaac Rosenbaum; Rabbi David Aharon Reisman, and all their families.

Reb Shlomo Gedalowitz was in one of the cars – without his family. Now too, as he had throughout his entire life, he was busy helping his fellow Jews. In a place where it was every man for himself, and all thought was to one's own survival, Reb Shlomo found the strength to offer a drink or more breathing space, to revive whoever needed it...and to remove anyone whose spark of life had been extinguished.

The train reached Auschwitz, and the Jews were forced out, those, that is, who were able to move.

Everyone was traumatized by the unbearable journey. Family members sought one another, wanting to be together again, when suddenly a thunderous silence fell over the group. A figure descended from one of the cars. There wasn't a single person who didn't recognize her. Her name was known to every resident of Bilke, and not for the good.

It was Miriam, the milkman's daughter.

Her parents were no longer alive. They were among the first hundred people to be taken to the Ukrainian forest and slaughtered. No one knew what had happened to their daughter. As far as they were concerned, the minute she betrayed her people, she was, for all intents and purposes, dead.

Rumors had reached them that her husband had quickly shown his true colors and begun to treat her like the rest of the non-Jewish husbands treated their wives, including the occasional beating. Yet since she'd move to a nearby village that had no Jews, they'd almost forgotten about her.

And now, here she was. Even if she had wanted to escape her Jewish origins, the Nazis didn't let her. The fact that she was married to a non-Jew didn't help, and she was taken like a sheep to the slaughter along with the rest of the Jews. What broke her spirit was the fact that her husband had done nothing to rescue her, but even seemed happy to get rid of her and her children – his children. When they'd shoved her onto one of the wagons, he hadn't said a word of protest.

Now she was walking numbly, all eyes upon her. Next to her walked her three children, a boy and two girls.

Everyone cried, and the women hugged her warmly, as if she'd never left the fold, as if she'd returned to them of her own free will.

Someone else got off the train, bringing the crowd to stunned silence. It was the gentile pharmacist of Bilke. He actually was a pharmacist, but he'd never been a goy.

Yet no one knew that. Yes, the Nazis managed to return to Judaism even those the Jews hadn't succeeded in bringing back.

They didn't have much time to wonder about it, though, because a few minutes later the Jews of Bilke met up with the dreaded Mengele, who decided their fate, sending some to life and others to death.

Half the Jews of Bilke were sent to the gas chambers on the holiday of Shavuos, and most of those who weren't lost their lives due to the slave labor and starvation, illness, and Nazi torments.

When the war ended, only a few dozen worn and broken survivors were left out of the thousands of Jews in Bilke. Among them was Reb Shlomo Gedalowitz.

❋ ❋ ❋

You need to understand what it was like then. An entire nation of people went up in flames, and those who were left were like burnt embers. They wandered like moving shadows, finding it hard to believe what they'd been through. The past was erased as if it had never been, and no eye could see the future.

Reb Shlomo found himself returning to Bilke. Most of the survivors had no place to go, so they returned to their homes – only to discover that there was no home. The structure might have been standing, but it was now inhabited by gentiles who had taken over their businesses and possessions as well. The Nazis, the Hungarians, and the locals completely destroyed everything Reb Shlomo's father had built – the large, magnificent shul, the *mikveh*, the guesthouse, the Talmud Torah, and all the other smaller shuls – leaving not a trace. Such was the fate not only of Bilke, but of all the villages, towns, and cities across Poland and Hungary.

"How come you weren't burned up with the rest of them?" former neighbors asked any Jew who had managed to stay alive.

That's why most of the Jews, after their traumatic return, quickly made their way to Eretz Yisrael, the United States, and any other place they could, as long as it was far away from the blood-soaked soil of Europe, that infamous land of evil and hatred.

Three days after Reb Shlomo returned, another person made his way back – a sixteen-year-old boy, Miriam's son Henrik.

Shlomo befriended him, making sure he had food and a place to stay. He discovered a confused young man, a Jew by birth who considered himself a gentile, a child whose life and soul had been destroyed by the past year's events. Suddenly, the boy found out that he belonged to the people he'd always despised. His own father turned his back on him and was unmoved at his being taken away to certain death. He'd experienced the death of his mother and two sisters, without any belief to hold onto.

Shlomo knew it was only a matter of time before this boy, with no other choice, would return to the nearby village in which he'd grown up and rejoin his father, even with all the anger and confusion he felt toward him. He knew that if this happened, the last remaining spark of the family would be extinguished forever.

Shlomo took care of the boy like a son, which he would have done in any event, but which now took on more urgency. At the same time, he developed connections with members of the Jewish Agency and arranged for them to get the boy to Eretz Yisrael as fast as possible.

The boy made aliya, was absorbed by a kibbutz in the north of the country, and quickly identified with the Jewish part of himself, despite there being no signs of religion at the kibbutz.

Shlomo personal plans were different. He decided to stay in Bilke and rebuild.

❋   ❋   ❋

Shlomo remarried. His wife was Golda Malka Eisdorfer from the neighboring village of Seredne. Two children were born to them, a boy and a girl, Yisrael Dov and Perel.

Survivors of the community, one from a city and two from a family, trickled in until some twenty-five people found their way back to their homes and property in Bilke. Not that they had it easy. The Russians, may their names be blotted out, robbed and cheated them out of all their belongings and took away everything.

In Bilke, Reb Shlomo started to rebuild the shul, the *mikveh*, and the guesthouse despite knowing full well that the chances of hosting numerous guests were virtually nil, at least for the next few decades or so.

With the fall of the Iron Curtain, dividing Europe into east and west, Bilke became part of the communist bloc, making fulfillment of Reb Shlomo's dream even harder. The communist government harassed and persecuted Jews, forbidding all religious activity under penalty of death.

Matzos were baked in stealth, and clandestine prayer services were held in the home of Reb Shlomo's brother Meir. When the Russians came searching during prayers, the Jews quickly dispersed, while the little children, Yisrael Dov and Perel, hid under the tables.

❄   ❄   ❄

At a certain point, Reb Shlomo Gedalowitz and his wife Golda Malka realized that their dream of raising an exemplary Jewish family was endangered. They took the highly unusual step of sending their children, Yisrael Dov and Perel, to relatives in America, and there they received a Jewish education.

Yisrael Dov and Perel grew up and established homes faithful to Torah and Judaism. Perel married Reb Avraham Fried, an Israeli who had immigrated to New York in the 1950s. The children born to them are all Torah- and mitzvah-observant.

In 1976, Reb Shlomo Gedalowitz came to the realization that his dream of restoring Bilke would remain just that, a dream. He and his wife, Golda Malka, finally immigrated to America, joining their children and grandchildren.

Reb Shlomo Gedalowitz passed away on 3 Adar 1980. His wife, Golda Malka, continued to enjoy great *nachas* from her children, grandchildren, and great-grandchildren.

❈   ❈   ❈

And now, Mr. Walder, here's how the story connects to you!

Fifteen years ago, your father, Reb Shlomo Walder of Haifa, traveled to New York to participate in the wedding celebration of his sister's daughter, Tova Mendelowitz.

During the week of *sheva berachos*, he bumped into Mr. Avraham Fried, Perel's husband. It turned out that Mr. Fried had learned in your father's yeshivah, Yeshivas Tiferes Yisroel, in Haifa.

Mr. Fried expressed a desire to contribute to the yeshivah in memory of his father, Reb Ephraim Shlomo, *z"l*, and his father-in-law, Reb Shlomo Gedalowitz, *z"l*. Soon after, he donated the magnificent shul on the yeshivah's second floor, which serves as the *beis midrash* of the *yeshivah ketanah* headed by Rabbi Ginsberg under the leadership of Rabbi Simcha Zissel Shapira, *shlita*.

Nor was this the end of Mr. Fried's generosity. A year ago, he again approached your father and asked to memorialize his father-in-law in a way that would somehow fulfill his dream of restoring Jewish life to Bilke, a dream he'd never been able to realize. Your father suggested that he donate a study hall and a guesthouse in the yeshivah.

And this Shabbos, *parashas Matot-Masei*, Mr. Avraham Fried, his wife Perel, and his mother-in-law, Golda Malka, will be guests in Haifa to celebrate the dedication of the hall, the mezuzah installation ceremony an hour before Shabbos, and the Shabbos *seudah* itself, because during the Three Weeks no festive event may be held on a weekday.

❈   ❈   ❈

Now for the fitting climax. What's my connection? Why am I telling you this whole story?

Because there's someone you might have forgotten: Henrik, Miriam's son.

Remember Miriam, the milkman's daughter who married a goy? Thanks to Reb Shlomo Gedalowitz, Henrik made aliya to Eretz Yisrael and lived on a kibbutz. He's not religious, and his children weren't raised to be, either. But one of them traveled to India after her army service, was religiously inspired there, and became *frum*.

Unbelievably, Henrik, my father, wasn't opposed to it. He said that his mother's parents deserved to have one branch continue their legacy. After my return to Judaism, I wanted to find out more about my family's history, especially the person who saw to it that Miriam did not leave her faith and that her son was not lost among the goyim. I quickly discovered Reb Shlomo Gedalowitz, Perel, Avraham Fried, and your father – whose name is also Shlomo, Shlomo Walder.

I won't be there at the ceremony because I don't think it's in my family's best interests for me to disclose our connection with this sensational story. But tell the story I must – for my poor grandmother Miriam; for my great-grandparents Reb Isaac Hersh and his wife, who died thinking their family's branch of the Jewish tree was cut off; for the *kedoshim* of Bilke; and for my hero, Reb Shlomo Gedalowitz.

15

Lost Learning, Lost Earning

I learned in a top yeshivah, where I was considered one of the best boys, a real *masmid*. When I was ready to build my own home, I quickly became engaged to a girl from an excellent family who is my wife till this very day.

Two weeks after our engagement, our parents started to look for an apartment for us. From time to time, they'd ask us to look at an apartment with them, but we didn't find anything we liked.

Almost two months later, we were all feeling the pressure. With the wedding only a month away, there was still no apartment in sight.

I'm not one to sit around and wait for things to happen; I make them happen. I was getting the distinct impression that everyone else was too busy to remember this crucial necessity. They were so caught up with the million and one details of making the wedding – the color scheme, the menu, the flowers – that they seemed to forget that after the party was over, we were supposed to be living somewhere.

One morning, I decided to take care of it myself.

I left in the middle of first *seder*, at 12:30 p.m., and headed for a realtor's office.

I sat with the realtor and he suggested various apartments until we narrowed it down to a few places that seemed right in terms of location, size, amenities, and price.

I told him that I wanted to see the apartments together with my *kallah* and both sets of parents. He said that wouldn't be a problem and that I should let him know when we wanted to see them. Then he had me sign a document that stated that if I did buy one of the apartments he showed me, I'd pay him 2 percent of the price as his fee, which is the going rate in the Israeli real estate market.

I got back to the yeshivah in time to daven Minchah, planning to call my parents so they could set up a time when we could all look at apartments that night. Before I got a chance to make the call, my future father-in-law called me at the yeshivah pay phone and said he'd spotted a notice tacked onto a tree advertising an apartment for sale that sounded like just what we were looking for.

"Great!" I said. "I also heard about some apartments today, but of course it's better to see the one you found because there's no realtor's fee to pay. Let's take a look at that one first."

We all met at nine o'clock, as planned, and went to the apartment listed on the piece of paper my father-in-law had torn off the tree. We saw the apartment and liked it.

"I don't think there's any reason for us to look at the apartments the realtor suggested," my father-in-law said.

I agreed. This apartment was perfect for us.

My parents and my *kallah*'s parents sat down with the owner, and the first question he asked was, "How did you know about the apartment, from a realtor or an ad?"

"I tore off the number from an ad tacked onto a tree," my *shver*-to-be said. "Here's the note."

Suddenly I got a sinking feeling. "Wait a minute." I took out the contract I'd signed with the realtor that morning, and when I saw what was written there, I felt terrible.

The first apartment listed was the apartment we were sitting in. I looked again. The same street, building, floor, and family. One plus one could only equal two.

I didn't know how to tell them, but I had no choice. In front of everyone – my parents, my parents-in-law, and my *kallah* – I was forced to admit that I'd gone to a realtor that morning and signed a contract promising him 2 percent if I bought this apartment, the very same apartment whose information my father-in-law had come across at that very same moment and torn off a tree.

I don't remember how much we lost on my *bitul Torah* that day, but you can figure it out. Two percent of an apartment in Jerusalem – that's the amount I would have saved if I had decided to sit and learn until the end of first *seder* instead of worrying about realtors. But I didn't pass the test, and we were forced to pay the realtor the entire amount.

I don't know which was harder, losing the money or having to tell that particular group of people, those closest to me, that I'd left in the middle of first *seder*. Anyway, it all adds up to the lesson I learned that day about *bitul Torah*.

❋   ❋   ❋

I know you like stories with a happy ending, so here's one for you. Years later, when I was learning in *kollel*, I had $20,000 saved up. I wanted to invest it and have it earn some money.

At that time, a lot of my friends were buying land near Ashkelon for $25,000 per unit. Hundreds of people who heard about it by word of mouth, including not a few *chareidim*, bought a plot after hearing that the land would be rezoned for residential construction within six months, which would increase its value ten times over.

The person marketing the land was a man alluded to quite frequently in your stories, but it could be that even you don't know about this. The reason everyone ran after him to buy land was because he was a well-known, respected figure with close ties to the community of *avreichim*. In fact, his recommendation was like a certificate of guarantee for the whole project. This same person acted in all innocence, believing that he was helping *avreichim* marry off their children easily.

I planned to invest in the project and had already talked about it several times with this contact person. I made up with him that I'd bring him the money. I had $20,000 and was missing $5,000, which I hoped to cover with a bank loan. My problem was the bank's opening hours. The bank opens at 8:30 a.m., and at that time I was learning in a *kollel* outside the city, which meant I had to leave for *kollel* much earlier than that.

The bank stayed open until 6:30 p.m. one day a week, and I planned to get to it then. But that same day I got stuck in traffic and by the time I got to the bank, the doors were closed.

The contact man started to pressure me. "There are only a few lots left," he said. "I'm saving one for you, but I can't promise."

I considered leaving for *kollel* half an hour later than usual, but then I remembered the promise I'd made to myself way back then, before my wedding. I said I'd never cancel Torah learning for mundane matters, even if it involved buying or selling an apartment or making a profit.

It wasn't an easy decision for me to make. Losing out on this deal wasn't an option. Everyone knew that it would set you up to marry off two or three children without going into debt. Everyone I knew was buying. Only I was stuck because of a $5,000 gap and a contact man who thought I wasn't playing straight with him.

"I heard you were a serious guy," he said in a tone that questioned just that. I squirmed, feeling totally irresponsible.

How can I lose out on such an opportunity? I asked myself. I had no good answer.

But missing *kollel* to take care of this deal was out of the question. I didn't dare. Sure, I'd been late on occasion when I'd had to take one of the kids to a doctor, but for money, never. I'd already learned my lesson the hard way.

I waited impatiently for the next Wednesday, the only day the bank was open late enough for me to make it. This time, I got in before the doors closed, and I got my $5,000 loan.

As soon as I walked out of the bank, I called the contact man to arrange a meeting. He didn't answer. I called again and again, sort of in shock that he wasn't answering, but at the same time knowing that I'd lost my chance to buy into the deal. He had never before not picked up a call from me.

That night, I went to his house and knocked on the door. When the door opened, I told him that I'd brought all the money and that I wanted to close the deal.

He looked at me, and it struck me that he didn't look like his usual self. "Let me ask you something," he said. "Are you the only person in the world who didn't hear the news?"

"What news?"

"The owner of the land flew the coup. He's no longer in the country. I have no idea where he is, either. All I know is that he declared bankruptcy. Not only that, but it turns out that the land wasn't exactly his.

"You don't know what I'm going through. Everyone's on my back, and they've got a point. I gave my word. Because of me, lots of *avreichim* lost their money. I really trusted him. I didn't want to listen to everyone who warned me not to do business with him. You've got a lot to be grateful for. Hashem saved you from losing your money."

I walked away stunned. Part of me wanted to dance right there in the street, but I didn't because so many of my friends had lost a lot of money. Some of them had taken out loans to buy a few plots of land.

On the way home, I went into a shul to daven Ma'ariv and said a special prayer of thanks for the resolution I'd made never to interrupt my learning unnecessarily.

Now I looked back at the money lost to the realtor as *rebbe gelt*. I'd paid a high price to learn that lesson, but it was worth it. Thanks to sticking to my learning schedule no matter what, I'd not only been saved from losing the $15,000 I had in hand, I'd been saved from borrowing more and falling into debt.

Now let me tell you where you come in. The man who went bankrupt had begun building a shul and couldn't finish it. The neighborhood children used to tease his son that his father hadn't finished what he'd begun. You wrote about it in the story "A Night in the Niche" in *Kids Speak* 4. Later they turned the story into a play.

I guess I wasn't the only one who didn't lose out from this unfortunate incident.

16

Like Olive Shoots around Your Table

I was born with a silver spoon in my mouth, as they say, and grew up that way too, in one of Jerusalem's finest neighborhoods. My parents are wonderful people who loved us kids and gave us everything we needed and more. We were given love, respect, and more love. We grew up in an ideal home environment and the results were as you'd expect. We all turned out just the way our parents wanted us to.

My father worked for a living, and my mother was a stay-at-home mom. Our income was always above average. We never delved into our parents' affairs, certainly not to ask, "Where's all the money coming from?" But as we grew older we came to understand that the big money came from various inheritances, and the biggest money came from investments. That's what made our parents well-off and perhaps even more than that. In addition to his job, my father ran a private loan *gemach* from the *ma'aser* money his investments brought in. This *gemach* was his pet project, and he put a lot of time and energy into running it.

We lived like royalty. My mother dressed us in nothing but the best, and no delicacy in the world fit for a king was missing from our Shabbos table. We were used to a luxurious, pampered lifestyle.

When my older sisters were ready to get married, my father looked for boys who would be lifetime learners. He knew that to make this happen, he'd have to give an apartment and see to it that there were no financial pressures on the young couple. Such an arrangement carries a steep price tag, which my father paid in full.

None of the in-law parents demanded an apartment in Jerusalem. They were willing to settle for an apartment in one of the suburbs, in a project, but my father liked to quote the second half of verse 3 from *Tehillim* 128, "Your sons will be like olive shoots around your table." He'd always add, "Not just your sons, but your daughters as well." My father wanted his children to live near him, and he was willing to pay for it.

My brothers were outstanding learners and top boys in every way, but my father didn't take advantage of the situation. He agreed to each side paying half of an apartment in a project, and then added enough money of his own so the couple could live in Jerusalem. He didn't get any argument from the other side, as you can well imagine.

We all knew about my father's dream to have everyone live in Jerusalem. "You'll see," he'd say. "You'll all live near us. If you want to, that is." Given our financial situation, it sounded like a real possibility.

We watched as Abba's dream started to come true. Two boys and two girls got married, and then my brother was the fifth. The night after the engagement party, I had trouble falling asleep. My thoughts were racing. As I tossed and turned, I heard my father and mother talking about buying an apartment. I don't remember their exact words, but it was something like, "Our savings are almost gone," my mother said. "Don't forget we have another three children after this. At this rate, we won't have a thing left. Think about the future. We're not talking about sending them to live somewhere across the ocean. Let's compromise on a cheaper apartment close to Jerusalem. There are a few new projects only thirty minutes to an hour away. What's wrong with that?"

I heard my father answer, short and decisive. "We've already discussed this many times. The children are staying near us, period. Besides, what's all this talk about what will be? *Baruch Hashem*, we have enough money, and our investments are bringing in a nice return, so why should I give up the dream of having all the children live nearby?"

So... My parents bought that brother an apartment in Jerusalem too. I was eighteen. Everyone took it for granted that I would live in Jerusalem, as well. I think I was the only one who even considered a different option.

I kept my ears open. My antennae were pretty well attuned to my parents' conversations, and I picked up a lot. Let this be a warning to parents who think they're living in some kind of soundproof bubble. They're not. There'll always be that one sensitive kid in the family, and in our family, that was me.

My brother got married and settled into a nice apartment nearby. After a slightly worrisome delay, the sister directly above me got engaged.

By then, I was twenty-one, and since I'd known for a few years what was going on, I was the only one who sensed that my father was starting to feel pressure. I guessed that my parents' bank account was nearing empty. For my sister, my father had to compromise on a more distant neighborhood, but still, it was in Jerusalem.

A while after this sister's wedding, my siblings, both the married ones and those still at home, noticed a change. Not a big change, but a change nonetheless. They noticed that on

Shabbos, our mother started to count how many portions of food she'd made, so that it would be exact. Cheap fruit drinks became honored guests at our Shabbos table instead of our favorite cola and sodas. It went unspoken, but we all realized that Abba would no longer be able to fulfill his dream of having all his children live in Jerusalem.

And then it was my turn. I was deep into the *parsha*. I found the right one much quicker than I'd thought. Before both sets of parents met to finalize things, I talked to my father and mother. I told them that I understood the situation was not what it used to be and that it would be totally okay with me if they let me wander a bit further. Before my mother could get too excited about my brilliant idea, my father said, "Rafi, you've probably forgotten the famous rule, never look a gift horse in the mouth."

I couldn't refuse my father's generous offer, especially when I saw that my mother was okay with it. They bought us a nice apartment in Jerusalem. It needed some serious renovations, but we were very happy with it.

❋   ❋   ❋

A few months after my wedding, what we kids had sensed and feared became fact. My father was in deep financial trouble. His investments fell through one after the other, and he went from being wealthy to deeply in debt.

His loan *gemach* shrunk because his *ma'aser* money trickled to almost nothing. Sadly, too many people borrowed and didn't repay, sticking the *gemach* with the loss. My father always treated the money he lent as half-loan, half-gift anyway, so he never went after the delinquent borrowers – not by calling in their cosigners or by taking them to *beis din*. The result was that the *gemach* was virtually stopped in its tracks, illustrating for us in vivid color the words in *Tehillim*: "A *rasha* borrows and doesn't repay."

My father had put his heart and soul into that *gemach*, and it broke him to have to tell people there was no money and turn them away.

One day, I walked into the house on the way home from *kollel* and my mother's face said it all. Before I even asked her anything, she started to talk. She told me that they had run out of money. To marry off the twins, the last children still at home, they'd have to go into debt. For the first time in her life, my mother was getting to know the concept of "being in debt" from the other side of the fence.

She told me that she'd tried to convince my father to promise a little less, but Abba wouldn't hear of it. He said that if they were already going to be taking out loans, they'd go all the way.

Not long afterward, we heard some good news. Both of the twins were engaged. Abba had taken on himself extensive financial obligations. The main thing was that his dream was coming true. All his children, boys, girls, sons-in-law and daughters-in-law – and now a quickly growing number of grandchildren – would surround his table in Jerusalem like

Some time after the wedding of the second twin, my parents reached the point where they couldn't make payments on their loans. We kids knew nothing about it. We were busy with our own lives. They tried to cope with it quietly – and failed.

While my wife and I were busy with our growing family, my parents were feeling the crunch as they struggled to pay back their loans. When they couldn't keep up the payments, the bank started foreclosure proceedings on their apartment, on which they had taken out a second mortgage.

One fine day, their large, luxurious apartment – and it was large and luxurious by any standard – was sold, and they had to get out within a month. At this point, they could no longer hide it from us. They asked us to help them pack.

I remember as if it were yesterday watching the strong, financially comfortable father I'd always known, the father who gave and gave and gave, reduced to helplessly packing his belongings, not knowing where he was going.

We children were all *kollel* families, struggling to make ends meet. This type of thing is so much harder for people like us, who grew up with a very comfortable standard of living. We had no idea what to do.

❀   ❀   ❀

My parents looked for an apartment to rent, but the larger ones cost a fortune, which they didn't have, and the smaller ones... They just couldn't get used to the idea. "At least let me have enough space to have the whole family over," my father said plaintively.

One day, my mother came home with a small smile and carefully said to my father that she'd seen a large apartment that was brand-new and cheap. She started to describe the apartment and told him the price. Abba thought she was dreaming. You couldn't find a rental apartment that size in Jerusalem at that price. Then Ima threw the bombshell. The apartment wasn't in Jerusalem. It was in a community about half an hour's drive away.

Stunned silence followed her suggestion, and then my father started to cry. The tears had been building up for a long time, and now there was no escaping them.

He, who had dreamed his whole life of having his sons and daughters around his table like olive shoots; he, who had worked and promised and come through on his promises, and given and sacrificed for the dream... And now, the dream had blown up in his face. His children had surrounded his table, but now that table would be orphaned and he'd be forced into exile.

He was devastated. The pain was too big for him to contain, and he burst out into heart-wrenching sobs. And we knew nothing about any of this.

My mother decided that she wasn't giving in. They consulted with *daas Torah* and received a clear-cut answer. In material matters, the wife decides, ruled the *rav*. My father left the meeting in turmoil, but with *emunas chachamim* in his heart. That very same week, they rented a large apartment in Modi'in Illit.

One day, they surprised us. They called and said we were invited to come for Shabbos whenever we wanted, but not in Jerusalem. We were in total shock. We'd been in denial. Now reality stared us in the face. It was totally surreal. We knew there was no way all of us were going to continue to live comfortably in Jerusalem while our parents, who had done so much for us, were sent into exile, their dreams shattered. We all felt heavy guilt. I personally felt that I couldn't continue my life as usual with something like this going on.

Things came to a head at the housewarming party we made for my parents in their rented apartment in Kiryat Sefer. We all came and tried to pretend that it was life as usual. The pretense worked to some extent, but not for me. I couldn't bear to see my father pouring cheap fruit drinks for everyone.

A week later, I called a meeting of all my brothers and sisters and their spouses, no kids.

I began by quoting from the Gemara *Gittin* 58a: "Rav Yehudah said in the name of Rav, 'What does it mean when they say, "And they oppress a man and his house, a man and his heritage?"' … It once happened that a carpenter's apprentice had a master who needed to borrow money. The master wanted to divorce his wife and didn't have enough money to pay her *kesubah*.

"The apprentice lent his master the money, and then went and married his [master's] ex-wife. The master couldn't repay the loan, so the carpenter said, 'Come work as my servant. That way, you'll pay off your debt.'

"They [the carpenter and his wife, who was the master's ex-wife] would sit, eating and drinking, and he [the master] would stand there serving them as tears fell from his eyes into their cups.

"At that hour, the judgment was sealed for the destruction of the *Beis Hamikdash*."

I didn't need to explain it to them. They all got the point. Even though the story is different, it resonated with us. All at once, ideas flew thick and fast.

The consensus was that each couple should contribute a set amount monthly toward rental of a big apartment in Jerusalem, one at least the size of the one in Kiryat Sefer. An apartment like that runs to about ten thousand shekels a month. Now you know the size apartment we're talking about.

But I had a different idea, one that was totally revolutionary.

"I think it's crazy to put out 120,000 shekels every year for dozens of years, especially since we're all in the same boat, learning in *kollel*," I told the group. "That's basically what we get as a stipend. It's not only impossible, it's a big waste of money.

"What's the alternative?" they asked.

"We sell our expensive apartments in Jerusalem, each one of which is worth at least 2,000,000 shekels, and buy apartments in Kiryat Sefer. I priced apartments there, and they're about half the price of an apartment here. Each couple will contribute 350,000 shekels toward buying a villa in Kiryat Sefer for our parents, and we'll still have a few hundred thousand shekels left over to invest in another apartment. This way we'll being doing the right thing, repaying our parents' generosity, and we'll also be able to sit and learn with peace of mind thanks to the extra income from the second apartment we've each bought and rented out."

It wasn't an easy decision. A few people, especially brothers-in-law, found it hard to think of leaving Jerusalem, though there was no argument that this was the right thing to do.

I was the first to sell my apartment and move to Kiryat Sefer. After that, my older sister did the same, followed by two of my brothers. Over the next two and a half years, the whole family moved there. We bought a huge luxury villa for our parents – for the price of an apartment in Jerusalem. Most of us invested in a second apartment, and the two holdouts are considering it. We'd made a change that wasn't an easy one, but I can't tell you how happy we are and what it did for our guilty consciences. And you know what? For our finances too.

Almost every Shabbos finds us gathered around our parents' Shabbos table in their enormous living room, enjoying good food, sharing *divrei Torah*, and singing the way only a big, happy, united family can.

I look at my father and mother and see the joy on their faces, and know that their dream – the one they'd thought was shattered forever – was restored to life.

All of us – their sons, daughters, sons-in-law, daughters-in-law, grandsons, and granddaughters – are like olive shoots around their table.

17

The Light of the Moon

I don't know if my story is worth sharing, because it's just about a plain, ordinary woman. Still, I'm writing to you because I think a lot of people will be moved by it.

I grew up in a quiet home with quiet parents who were fairly "square." They were good people who worked hard but earned little. They didn't have any connections, so they didn't get any special treatment anywhere.

My parents had five children, and I'm the third, the middle child. Not that it made much difference. We were all pretty quiet, not troublemakers or bothersome.

My parents were each the only child in their family, so we didn't have a big, extended family. It was pretty much just us. Friends weren't in the picture, either, except for my father's friends from shul. There too, he wasn't too noticeable, being the youngest person there.

Try to imagine an unknown family without any connections. That was us. I didn't sense it as a child, but when I entered seminary it struck me how isolated we were. As I listened to my friends talking about their extended families, about their neighbors and their parents' friends, I realized that we'd been somehow left by the wayside. Not that there was any need to forget us, because we'd never been known in the first place.

Years later I realized that my siblings and I grew up on the fringes of society. What I mean is, we went to all the right schools, but we didn't have the personality or ability to form social connections. If anyone had asked about us, half the people would have said they didn't know us, and the other half would have said good things about us *because* they didn't know us.

I don't know how I managed to grow up in a family like that, with no friends, no social network, nothing that would make us stand out and give us our place.

My younger brother was a little different. He did manage to find his place socially. He even brought friends home, which was unheard-of in our house. And he succeeded in life far better than any of us. We paid the price for it, though, because once he realized that our family was what it was, he stayed with friends. When he got married, he settled down in a different town and made only one brief visit a year.

But I'm getting ahead of myself.

My two older brothers didn't get married until they were much older than the norm. I started *shidduchim* when I was twenty-three because I was waiting for them to get married first. They were the ones who insisted that I start going out. They said it wasn't so bad if a girl skipped over a boy.

My parents weren't involved because they had no idea how to go about it. How should they know who to ask or how to check out a boy or which yeshivah was good and which wasn't? They called up *shadchanim*, who said whatever they said, and believed them. Besides, they had no way of checking things out. I went out with two boys who didn't want me after the first meeting, and then I went out with a boy who did want a second meeting.

In retrospect, he wasn't a good match for me. But I didn't know it at the time. I didn't think there might be other boys out there more suitable for me.

He was different from my brothers and seemed to be a leader. I agreed to continue seeing him, though I didn't actually like him.

After a few meetings, we got engaged. At the engagement party, a lot of people from his side came, but I had only my small family. No neighbors, no friends...no nothing.

After the engagement, he started speaking against my parents. He said they were stupid and "totally not with it." I wanted to tell him that they might not be "with it," but that they weren't stupid. Instead, I kept quiet because I was the quiet type.

As the wedding drew closer, I discovered a few *middos* of his that were not all that great, but I didn't dream of saying anything to anyone.

After the wedding, my life became one big, long nightmare. He crushed me and disparaged me, humiliated me at every opportunity, destroyed my self-confidence, mocked me, worked me to the bone and never once said a word of thanks.

From a calm home where I'd never seen a single bad thing in my life, not ridicule and not cynicism, not shouting and certainly not hitting, I was thrown into a life I'd never known, with everything the opposite of what I'd been used to.

I found a good job in computers, and since I was good at what I did, I earned a nice salary. I gave the money to him, and he did with it as he pleased.

He'd get up late, maybe learn a little, but not work at all. Every minute he wasn't sleeping and wasn't away from home, he put me down and hurt me, and I put up with my shame in silence.

Two children were born to us, a girl and a boy. I was living an impossible life and didn't even know it.

When my son turned three and he started to hurt him too, I knew I had to do something, but I had no idea what.

When my son was four, I "happened" to attend a course for personal empowerment. Of course, there's no such thing as chance. A woman there related something that had happened in her life. We all identified with her, but I realized that what she had told wasn't even a tenth of what I and my children were going through. At the end of the evening, I went over quietly to the person who gave the series of lectures, a very gentle, spiritual *rebbetzin*, and hesitantly told her that I thought there might be something wrong with my home life. She gave me her time and attention. I cried and told her everything that was happening to me. She looked shocked. She couldn't believe that such a thing could be happening. When I finished, she encouraged me and asked my permission for her husband, the neighborhood *rav*, to speak with my husband.

I wasn't sure it was a good idea, but she told me that nothing could be worse than what I was going through already.

When the *rav* called him in for a talk, my husband had no idea what the conversation was going to be about. When he came home, he was all fire and brimstone. I don't want to describe what took place, but calling it a frenzied rampage would be putting it mildly.

I was afraid to go back to the *rebbetzin* and tell her what had happened, but she was smart enough to come to my house. She wanted to see for herself how I was feeling.

The *rav* and his wife got several community *askanim* involved. They made several attempts to put things in order, but they found my husband to be a tough man who wasn't willing to hear about getting help, let alone changing.

One day, he told me he'd opened a file in *beis din* to get a divorce. At first, I felt terrible. But the *rav* and *rebbetzin* encouraged me not to oppose it, and I became a divorcée.

Three very hard years followed. I was alone. My poor parents didn't know what to do with me. The situation had them so worried and confused. I continued to work, and finally the money had a good purpose. I put it into my children and my home. But I still felt like the loneliest, most pitiful woman in the world.

The *rav* and *rebbetzin* stood by me. They invited me to their home, and they kept up an ongoing interest in my life. The *rebbetzin* was always very supportive.

Eventually, they began to suggest *shidduchim*. I met a few divorcées, and they weren't for me. Life had taught me enough so that I could pick up on subtle behaviors and know what to expect.

And then they suggested a widower who was older than I by a dozen years. I hesitated at first, but the *rebbetzin* encouraged me to give it a try. We met, and it was like stepping into a different world. I'd never met anyone like him.

He was so *good*. He was smart, relaxed, full of empathy, interesting, fascinating even. His questions showed the depth of his understanding, and his responses testified to the depth of his humanity. After the first meeting, I prayed that he would want to continue.

He did, and after four meetings, he proposed. I agreed right away, and the wedding date was set for six weeks later. It was a small ceremony, and from that moment on, my life changed.

At his suggestion, we sent the children to stay with my parents for the first month. His children were old enough – one was even married – to manage by themselves.

We spent that month up north. That month was a purification of all the bad I'd gone through in my life. I told him everything. He listened and listened, and after I unburdened myself, he started to build me up.

How? With words. He told me how he saw me and how he viewed my strengths. He praised me and said how special I was, how good and pleasant, how smart and hardworking, how I was always smiling, how I was so kind and gentle – and hundreds of other compliments I'd never heard before, not from my parents and certainly not from my first husband.

I was suspicious at first. I thought he was just saying these things to make me feel better. Then it dawned on me that he sincerely meant what he said. *Okay,* I thought, *he believes it, but one day he'll realize that he's got it wrong.*

That never happened. He was full of warmth and love and kind words. I realized why his children had turned out to be so special, so warm and relaxed, so accepting of me as a mother despite the short time they'd had to get used to me.

We wound up that magical month and returned home, with his children and mine, and started to build a family. I don't know how a lottery winner feels, but I know for sure I felt even better.

From a solitary existence, with no identity, recognition, or warmth, I was suddenly thrust into a joyously wonderful life that I can't even begin to describe. I was now blessed with a wonderful husband who was smart, attentive, gentle, good- hearted, helpful, generous, and again generous and again and again. His children were adorable, and like him, kind and good, easygoing and not critical, happy with what they had, despite their sadness over their beloved mother's death after an illness.

I promised myself I'd make it up to them, and I tried. Every morning, I got up early to make them breakfast, pack their lunches and snacks, and prepare their clothing. I helped them with their homework and did my best to take care of all their needs. I paid attention to how they were feeling. No matter how much I did, though, I still felt that I could never give them enough for all the joy I'd received.

It's hard to describe the gift I received, especially since it was so unexpected. Me, who never even knew of the existence of such a life, was suddenly handed it as a gift.

My two children blended in with his children as if they'd always been part of that family. They became bright, sociable, happy kids.

Now we're about to marry off one of my husband's children, who is like a daughter to me in every way. I was at her side throughout all the meetings, the *vort*, the engagement, the shopping and all preparations, and then, unexpectedly, she left me a letter. I don't have the right to share what was written, but it was filled with so much love and appreciation and acceptance of me as her mother in every way, that my happiness levels shot up sky-high.

Over the years, my two brothers got married and had children. My husband brought them close to our family circle, and it's impossible not to see the good effect this closeness has on them.

I like to quote the verse from Yeshayahu that says, "And the light of the moon shall be like the light of the sun," because to me, this says it all. We were a family that was forgotten, like a moon eclipsed.

I'm not joking. That really describes us.

And then suddenly, my husband and his family appeared, like a bright sun that shone on us, lighting us all and turning the pale light of the moon into the light of the sun.

The moral of my story is obvious, but I'll spell it out anyway. Plenty of people start off with what I have now, but they don't know how to appreciate it because they think it's the norm.

And a moral that's no less major: look at the power of one single person to give life, happiness, and warmth to another person and the world! My husband is my rescuing angel. He rescued my soul from prison and brought me – and my children, and all the generations to come forth from us – to a world of joy and light. I owe him so much.

I'll be devoted to him for the rest of my life, with gratitude and a prayer in my heart that Hashem bless him with strength, health, and *nachas* until 120 for the great light he brought from his sun to the pale light of an eclipsed moon that was my fate in the past.

18

Lost and Found

I live in a well-known city in the center of the country. A few years ago, one of the city's residents retired and chose to receive his pension money in a lump-sum payment. He changed his shekels to dollars – getting $170,000, to be exact – with which he planned to buy a second apartment to rent, which would give him a steady income.

He was approved for a mortgage of several hundred thousand shekels, and on the day of signing on the apartment, he took all his cash in a large brown envelope, hailed a cab, and set out to meet the lawyer.

On the way, a secretary from the lawyer's office called him and said they were missing a document. He insisted they had it. The secretary searched while he waited and then said she couldn't find it. He said that when he got there he'd go over the file and show them that the document was there among all the other papers.

Naturally, he was tense, and asked the driver to hurry. When they reached the building where the lawyer had his office, he handed the driver a fifty-shekel bill, which was ten shekels more than the fare, and said, "Keep the change. I'm in a rush."

He flung open the door and raced to the building. Suddenly, he remembered that he'd forgotten something in the cab.

That something was a package with $170,000!

He ran after the cab, but had to stop after it turned down a side street and disappeared. There was no point chasing it. He tried to think of a way to contact the driver. It dawned on him that he had no idea who the driver was or what the name of the company was. He didn't even know what kind of car it was, only that it was white.

❀　　❀　　❀

He dashed into the lawyer's office only to be told that they'd found the missing document, the sellers were already there, and the contract could be signed. That's when they noticed that he was hysterical.

"Give me the phone!" he cried. "I left all the money and mortgage papers in the cab."

The whole office – the lawyer, secretary, and even the sellers – rallied to the cause. They called all the taxi companies in the city and asked their dispatchers to ask the drivers if anyone had found a package.

The answers came quickly, one after the other. No one reported finding it.

The lawyer called the taxi companies again and asked them to try to find a driver who had driven to that address or that area. They said they'd check, but they seemed reluctant to accuse one of their own drivers.

The man who lost his money felt like his world had caved in. He collapsed right there in the lawyer's fancy office. An ambulance was called, but the EMTs said it was an understandable reaction and there was no need to transport him to the hospital. They stayed with him a short time, as did the lawyer and even the sellers, who, though they knew the deal was off, at least for that day, didn't have the heart to leave the buyer in that state after he'd lost so much money.

Finally, somehow, he recovered. A family member came to drive him home, both because of his emotional state and because taking a taxi didn't seem like such a great idea after what had happened.

In the days that followed, he left no stone unturned trying to track down the taxi driver. He called all the companies and asked if any of their drivers had found a large sum of money. They all said no. A few of them added that if none of their drivers had told them about it that same day, the chances of him ever seeing the money again were zero, because along with the money, the package contained the mortgage papers, which identified the owner of the money better than a thousand witnesses. If someone had wanted to return the money, they would have already found a way to do so.

The man was starting to lose hope of ever seeing his money again. He knew he had to keep going, but anguish over the loss robbed him of any desire to start a new job. You might say he sunk into a mild depression that left him too drained to go on with life.

And then a friend suggested that he go to a *rav* in Bnei Brak to get a blessing.

He went.

The *rav* listened patiently to his story, and sympathized with him.

"The person who found the money is not a thief," he said, "but the moment he opened the envelope and saw your name and contact information, he became one. He knows it, and his conscience is surely troubling him. You need to make some sort of effort so that Hashem will make the man regret his action, if he hasn't already spent the money."

"What does the *rav* suggest?" the man asked.

"I suggest that you do something to bring merit to the masses. We call this *zikui harabbim*. Get as many people as possible to learn Torah, and if Hashem wills it, you'll see salvation. If not, you will be blessed with an abundance of blessing in other ways. In any case, you will have the strength to return to your activities, which is more important than anything, even money."

The man left the *rav*'s house in confusion. He was a simple person, not *frum*. He knew what Torah is, but he had no idea what the *rav* meant by bringing "merit to the masses."

He went back to the friend who had sent him to the *rav* and asked, "Let me ask you something. What is this *zikui harabbim* thing? How do you do it?"

"It's like this," the friend said. "If you cause people to do mitzvos or stop transgressing, that's *zikui harabbim*."

"The *rav* mentioned learning Torah," the man recalled.

"Wonderful!" his friend said. "Organize an evening. Invite a speaker. That's a great way to bring merit to the masses."

"I'll think about it," the man said and went home.

The next morning, he woke up knowing what he was going to do. A year earlier, he had attended a lecture given as part of an all-day Torah program in his neighborhood. Now that he understood what bringing merit to the masses meant, he had a brainstorm. He'd make an all-day, all-night Torah event on the fifth of Iyar, the anniversary of the day in which Israel's independence was proclaimed. It would run from 8:00 a.m. to 8:00 a.m. the next day.

He started immediately. Most lecturers were booked for that day, but he was determined. He told them he would pay for transportation as well as the speech they gave. Slowly but surely the time slots were filled in, and then he started calling the big names. They told him they were booked up for the fifth of Iyar for the next four years.

"Listen to the hour I want you for, and you'll see you're not booked for it."

"Okay," they said. "When do you want me to speak?"

"Between three and four in the morning," he told one.

"What makes you think I'm not sleeping at that time?"

"I'm sure you are, but once you hear my story, I think you'll agree to come."

He told each of them the story of the lost $170,000 and the *rav*'s advice to him to do something to benefit the public. "I'm asking you to please give me this hour of your time, for full payment, of course."

The story attracted public interest and drew the lecturers as well. They all wanted to help him, and waived their travel expenses. They willingly gave up their sleep to help him achieve his goal, and a day before the date, the schedule was filled up with close to twenty lecturers.

He advertised extensively in his city and the surrounding area. The project generated a lot of excitement, in part because of its rarity. Not every day does a private individual make an all-day Torah event in a wedding hall, complete with refreshments. Add to this that the story behind it started to become public knowledge, especially among the seventeen- to twenty- two-year-old crowd, some of whom were on the streets but who felt bad for the poor guy who'd lost so much money.

On the fifth of Iyar, Shacharis took place at 8:00 a.m. on the dot, followed by the first lecture, with some two hundred people in attendance. With each passing hour, more people came, until by the afternoon, about eight hundred people filled the hall, listening to the talks and lectures and enjoying the coffee, cakes, and hot buffet.

At night, the youth started to pour in. Instead of wandering the streets with nothing to do, they were drawn to the brightly lit hall.

By 10:00 p.m., all the taxis in the city and surrounding area were busy bringing people to the event. In each taxi sat four or five youths with white *kippahs* on their heads who told the driver they were going to a Torah marathon. Most of them knew the story behind it – that a man had lost his money in a taxi. And they all had plenty to say, none of it pleasant, about the driver who had stolen the money. They also had plenty of ideas about what he'd done with it. None of them thought he'd wasted it or spent it frivolously. Most thought the money had gone to medical expenses or some other desperate need.

After hearing the story, most of the taxi drivers added their "best wishes" to the driver who stole the money and ruined the life of a passenger. They had a few choice words too, for the way he was ruining the good name of taxi drivers everywhere. Not that their reputation was the greatest to begin with. It was only slightly lower than that of Knesset members and journalists. And when a taxi driver sends this type of "best wishes," believe me, we're talking about the number one expert in delivering that type of "blessing," which made that taxi driver one of the most cursed men that night.

By twelve midnight, some two thousand people filled the hall. Taxis streamed to the place, bringing more and more young people out for a good time. Once they entered the hall, though, the serious atmosphere quieted them down, and they sat and listened. Time passed, and before you knew it, it was three o'clock in the morning, time for the most popular speakers.

By dawn, there were 2,500 people in attendance.

And then, a minute before the last speaker, I went over to the organizer and asked to be allowed to address the crowd.

He looked at me and seemed to catch my look of excitement. Realizing I must have something important to say, he gave his consent.

I went up on stage.

"I've been here only since midnight," I said into the microphone, "which is when I heard about this event and the reason behind it.

"Like everyone else here, I've listened to the talks. All the speakers spoke about our ability to do *teshuvah*. Allow me to talk about the man who took the money."

A hush fell over the crowd.

"There's a prayer we say every day: 'Please don't test me.' Everyone sitting here has mentally or verbally cursed the person who took the money. But did anyone consider the test he faced when he found $170,000 in his taxi? Try to find a point in his favor. He didn't break into the man's house and steal. He found a package in his taxi. Maybe he was under a lot of financial pressure, and didn't pass the test. Maybe he gave in to a fleeting temptation and told himself that the person who lost the money was a multimillionaire who wouldn't even feel the loss."

The crowd hung on my every word.

"I want to tell you what happened to the person who found the money," I said. "He was a hired driver for a private taxi. That means he wasn't connected to any company. The owner of the taxi had a two-way radio installed that picked up dispatches from all the companies. That's how he was able to snag customers. The driver had to pay a lot of money to the owner each month for the privilege of driving this taxi, leaving him with barely enough to get by, and often not even that.

"He didn't stand up to the temptation. He took the money. He didn't use it. He just put it in his house. It gave him a feeling of security, but his conscience didn't let him use the money.

"Like all of us here, he heard about this all-day, all-night Torah event. A few days later, he heard about the reason behind it. His guilty conscience gave him no peace. He walked around numbly, not knowing what to do. Part of him wanted to return the money – and part of him wanted to keep it.

"He's been driving his taxi tonight, bringing people here. Like the other taxi drivers, he heard plenty from his passengers about what they think of the person who took the money. As if that wasn't enough, he heard on his two-way radio exactly what the other taxi drivers thought of that person. He was scared. Even if he wanted to return the money, how could he? And more important, did he want to return it?

"At midnight, he called me. We've been close friends for years. He was broken, and asked me what to do.

"I asked him to bring me to the event and said I'd try to talk to the man who had organized it.

"I've been sitting here listening to the speakers since 12:30, and I've been very inspired. They spoke about the importance of learning Torah and doing mitzvos, about honesty and justice. And then the speaker before the last one talked about 'making a *kiddush Hashem*.'

"I called up the driver and we talked. I told him he had a chance to come out looking good both in Heaven's eyes and right here on earth. He could make a *kiddush Hashem*, with 2,000 people knowing that *zikui harabbim* had made him repent for his fall. He was convinced. Fifteen minutes ago, he called me. I went outside and he gave me this bag." I held up a black plastic bag. "I haven't opened it yet, but now, in front of this holy assembly, I will do so."

I opened the plastic bag and pulled out a big paper bag. It was open. I turned it upside down over the lectern and dollars rained down.

The audience was in shock. Someone escorted the organizer to the stage and said to him, "Count."

The bills were in bundles of ten thousand dollars each.

He started to count in front of everyone: "One, two, three... seven, eight, nine, ten."

The crowd joined him: "Eleven, twelve, thirteen, fourteen, fifteen, sixteen, seventeen."

All the money was there, right down to the last cent.

An unbelievable excitement swept through the hall. Twenty-five hundred people stood up and started singing and moving up to the stage, wanting to hug me and kiss me on each cheek. I can't describe how I felt after getting 2,500 bear hugs. I have even less to say about the kisses...

As I anticipated, lots of people suspected me of being the taxi driver, but it didn't seem to matter too much to them. Actually, they were the ones who gave the biggest hugs and the most kisses.

Pure happiness filled the air. You might say that it was really a feeling of *zikui harabbim*...

The organizer thanked everyone and then said, "I forgive with all my heart the man who took the money. All my pain and anguish are completely gone right now. They've been replaced by great happiness. I wish him all the best and want to ask all of you to wish him in your hearts only good. He's a real tzaddik who has repented, and where *ba'alei teshuvah* stand, even those who have never sinned can't stand."

A roar arose from the crowd and I again was subjected to a deluge of hugs, especially from those who thought I was the real tzaddik, the *ba'al teshuvah*.

Suddenly, in the midst of all these hugs, who do I see standing there but my friend, the taxi driver.

In the end, he decided to come, and it's a good thing he did. The outpouring of joy and happiness there, the spirit of forgiveness made him genuinely happy about what he'd decided to do. He realized then that he'd fixed what he'd damaged, and that now he was clean and pure and could continue living his life with a clear conscience.

That's the story, and I want to dedicate it to all the people who have fallen at one time or another, or who sense themselves slipping. No man is without sin, but the gates of repentance are never locked. If each of us would take it upon himself to fix at least one wrong we've done to our fellow man, it would be the perfect way to bring merit to the masses.

19

Gifts to the Poor

I've been a *ba'al teshuvah* for twenty years.

My past is far from worthy of admiration. And when I say far, I mean far. You want to know the truth? I'm ashamed of it. I used to terrorize people and even did time for it.

When I returned to my heritage, I left all that behind me. I became close with the rabbi of our neighborhood, who is a truly great man. I follow the path on which he guides me, and see blessing from it.

Last Purim, the rabbi gave a thousand dollars to each of thirty needy families in our neighborhood. Not many people knew how he came by so much money, but now, with his permission, I'm going to tell you the whole story.

It's not easy to be the rabbi of our neighborhood. I'll cut to the chase and just say that the disagreements he's asked to mediate aren't the usual ones about "I've got a neighbor who isn't talking to me." No, they're more physically oriented, if you get my meaning. Our neighborhood is full of people who are far from simple. We've got a lot of debts and a lot of problems here. But our rabbi, may he live and be well, can relate to everyone.

He talks to each person on his level, and tries to help him solve his problems. He'll do just about anything to help a fellow Jew.

One day, a man who lives in the neighborhood went to the rabbi for help. He told him he'd fallen into serious debt due to a family member's medical expenses.

Now, there's debt...and there's *debt*. He didn't owe money to the banks. Owing money to the bank is a wealthy man's problem, because wealthy people have a bank account, and the bank can go into that account or an account in another bank and take back the money it's owed. And if there's no money, there's an apartment. And if there's no apartment, there's a car. And if there's no car, there's a motorcycle. Are you following?

Poor people may have a bank account, but it's always frozen. And the bank can't take the apartment because it's only a rental, and they can't take the car because there is none... or selling it would cost more than it's worth. Then the bank throws up its hands in frustration and doesn't take them down.

The flip side of the coin is that when the bank sees someone who doesn't have any way of paying back a loan, they don't give him one. It's a fifty-fifty proposition: they don't loan to the poor, and the poor don't pay them back.

But when the bank won't give you a loan and you need the money, you may be driven to look for money in the gray market. Those shady characters there, why, you wouldn't believe how agreeable they are. Unlike those mean folks at the bank, they'll always give you a loan on the spot. They don't ask you any questions about earning ability, either, or use all kinds of fancy terminology their customers don't understand. Best of all, you don't have to sign any legal documents filled with small print... because not always do they understand even the large print.

These fellows in the gray market hibernate until half an hour – forget two or three days – after a loan payment is missed. Then they turn out to be a lot less agreeable than you thought. They want the debt repaid along with a "fine" of double, or four or five times as much. Let's not talk about petty things like carting off your table and chairs. And don't think they'll spend a penny on selling your old jalopy. Why waste time and money when, for the price of a gallon of gas, they can just set fire to the car itself?

And that's only the beginning. I suggest we skip the rest, for obvious reasons.

The fact is, that neighborhood resident came with a very sad tale of a five-thousand-dollar loan for urgent medical needs that ballooned into a massive debt of thirty thousand dollars.

"Who do you owe the money to?" the rabbi asked.

When he said the name, the rabbi knew he was in deep trouble. Over the years, he'd heard many stories of financial hardship from the people who came to him. He had even helped many of them, whether by soliciting donations or connecting them with the right charity fund. But this was a matter of life and death. This loan shark was known to be a violent man who didn't know the meaning of compromise. In the past, when people had tried to appeal to his conscience, in retaliation he had increased the payback amount.

"Listen, I understand your difficult situation," the rabbi said, "and I'm willing to contribute five hundred shekels of my own, even though my own financial situation is not all that great. But thirty thousand dollars is beyond what I can give."

"I know," the man said. "I didn't come here to get the money from you. I need your advice."

The man had a relative in France. Someone told the story to that distant relative, and he said he'd be willing to give ten thousand dollars, but he wanted a rabbinical figure to accept the money and to be the one to pay it directly to the creditor.

It was a brilliant idea. Apparently that distant French relative had a head on his shoulders and understood human nature. He didn't want the money to change hands unnecessarily where part of it or all of it might reach other hands, such as, for instance, those of the go-between and the relative who was in debt.

"What would I have to do?" the rabbi asked.

"I'll pay for your round-trip ticket to France," the man said. "You'll fly out early Sunday morning and return home the same day at seven in the evening. The whole thing will take sixteen hours of your time, which I know is precious. But you'll be rescuing me from a terrible situation."

The rabbi didn't think twice. Giving up a day in his life would take some doing because of his many obligations, but as far as he was concerned, it was for a very worthy cause.

Right after Shabbat, he headed for the airport to board an early morning flight to Paris. He landed at about 11:00 a.m.

As soon as he landed, the debtor called him. "Rabbi, you won't believe it," he said. "An hour after you boarded the plane I found out that my French relative has to make an urgent trip to Rome. I tried to call you, but you were already in the air."

The rabbi took a deep breath. The whole trip was for nothing. After all that trouble, the wealthy relative had just flown off.

"Everything is for the best," the rabbi said. "I'll have to return empty-handed."

"There might be one chance," the man said.

"Which is?"

"I don't know, but the flight to Italy leaves at twelve. Maybe you can meet him somehow in the terminal."

"That's a good idea," the rabbi said. "I'll wait here."

As soon as the conversation ended, the rabbi realized that it wasn't such a good idea because he still hadn't davened Shacharit. He'd planned to do so as soon as he got to Paris and found a minyan. Now he'd have to miss davening with a minyan. If he left the airport, he wouldn't be back within the hour. It was a real dilemma.

He thought about it long and hard, and when a Jew, even one who is himself a rabbi, isn't sure what to do, he goes to his *rav*.

His *rav* was none other than the renowned Torah giant Rav Yaakov Eidelstein, *shlita*.

He called the *Rav*'s home and posed the question.

"Go daven with a minyan in Paris," the *Rav* said, "and then return to meet him."

"With all due respect," the rabbi said, "I don't see how I'll be able to do both. Either I remain here at the airport and meet the man, or I go daven with a minyan and miss the meeting."

"Go daven, and Hashem will help you," Rav Eidelstein said.

The rabbi didn't think twice. He traveled to Paris, davened with a minyan, and then raced back to the airport. *I'll wait here until my return flight,* he told himself.

He hadn't taken more than two steps when suddenly a French Jew came over to him and said, "Are you the Israeli rabbi?"

"Yes, that's me."

"I want to apologize for disappearing on you like that at the last minute. It's an important meeting, arranged from one minute to the next, and I have to be there. You won't believe it, but the flight to Rome is delayed. I was sure you'd left the airport for Paris and didn't wait for me. Still, I looked for you, and I see that you remained here after all. I feel very upset that I was the cause of this confusion and delay. But don't worry. Your trouble won't be in vain. Because of your extraordinary effort, I'll increase the amount of my donation."

He pulled out his checkbook. "I'm filling this in for thirty thousand dollars to pay off the entire amount owed by my distant relative. I only ask you to see that it reaches the right person and to make sure my relative doesn't get himself in such a situation again."

The rabbi now faced a problem. He knew that he hadn't been waiting in the airport as the wealthy Frenchman assumed. He'd gone to Paris.

"It's not easy for me to say this," the rabbi began, "but I want to correct a misapprehension on your part. I didn't wait here for you all this time. I traveled to Paris and back. It's a miracle that you met me here."

The man shot him a startled look, and then turned pensive. "Now I truly stand in awe of you," the wealthy man said. "If I had any doubts, not that I did, now it's perfectly clear to me that you are a man of truth and that I can trust you. Do you know what? I'm sure it was hard for my relative to come up with the money to pay for your ticket, so I'll make out another check to cover that."

The rabbi told the wealthy man about his conversation with Rav Eidelstein, and repeated what Rav Eidelstein had told him: "Go daven and everything will turn out okay."

They parted in friendship, and the rabbi returned to Israel.

When he landed, he decided that he'd give the second check directly to the person who had paid for the ticket. Foremost in his mind was a desire to fulfill the wealthy man's request that the money be given directly, without intermediaries. At home, he picked up the phone to the travel agency that had issued the ticket and asked who had paid for it.

They gave him the name.

The minute the rabbi heard the name, he knew the whole business was not what he had thought. The person who'd bought the ticket was the loan shark, the one whose supposed threats had forced the whole trip.

Familiar as he was with all sorts of crooks and characters, the rabbi decided to check out the story one more time.

It didn't take him long. The man from his neighborhood who had come crying to him turned out to be a partner in crime with the loan shark. Together they had planned the sting operation on the French relative by fabricating a fake threat and danger that would tug at the wealthy man's heartstrings. Since the wealthy relative knew with whom he was dealing, he had asked for a Torah figure to vouch for the story's truth. The rabbi, who didn't know about the neighborhood resident's connections with the criminal, took pity on him and almost fell into the trap.

Almost.

If the rich man hadn't given the second check to cover the cost of the tickets, if the traveler to Paris hadn't gone to daven with a minyan and hadn't admitted the truth, he really would have fallen into the trap.

The rabbi didn't hesitate for a minute. He called the rich Frenchman and told him the whole story. The man was appalled. The rabbi suggested that he tear up the check, but he said. "Oh no. That money was given to charity, and it will stay that way. You will distribute it as you see fit to the poor in your neighborhood, and I take it there are plenty."

Now you know how thirty thousand dollars rained down on the poor people in the neighborhood, all of whom were handpicked by the rabbi, based on need. Hashem Himself gave gifts to the poor by way of His trustworthy representative, the neighborhood rabbi.

Actually, one other family deserved help, but the rabbi had no more money to distribute. I suggested that we collect from the families who had gotten the money.

"I'm not touching their money," the rabbi said. "I'll make a special fund-raising campaign."

That's the story, more or less. You're probably wondering where I come in.

Well, the wealthy Frenchman immediately called up his relative and told him he should forget that they were ever related. The loan shark was very unhappy with the rabbi's actions, and sent people to threaten him. He had them say that the rabbi owed him money (!) and that if he didn't bring it, there'd be a "present" waiting for him next to his house.

The rabbi decided to send his own present: me.

I went to the guy, who knew exactly who and what I was (better yet, who I had been). His tone changed. He asked me nice and polite what brought me to his doorstep and why I was getting involved. I told him that I wasn't getting involved in his loan business, despite what I thought of it. But seeing as he was trying to cheat my rabbi and was threatening him, that made it my business.

"Still, I brought you a peace offering," I told him, and handed him the amount he'd paid for the ticket. "This belongs to you, and the rabbi didn't touch it. I expect you to call the rabbi and ask his forgiveness."

He looked at me, and I returned the look with one from my past. And then he said, "Okay, tzaddik. Tell the rabbi that I take it back and that I ask his forgiveness. Tell him to give the money to charity. Okay?"

We shook hands, and I returned to the rabbi with another gift, this one for the last family on the list.

20

The Jewish Connection

I travel abroad on business frequently. My travels bring me into contact with many Jewish organizations, and I've participated in all sorts of Jewish activities around the globe.

This story began twenty years ago on one of my trips.

I was in a remote African country when I got a phone call from a friend asking me to go to the local hospital. He said a former Israeli IDF officer had been seriously injured on a trip and needed emergency care.

When I got to the hospital, I found a man who was broken both physically and mentally.

On a safari into the jungle, he'd climbed a tall tree. When the branch he was standing on broke, he fell to the ground, breaking both legs, several ribs, and fracturing his pelvis.

He had undergone several operations during which plates and screws were inserted to hold his bones together. A tall, strong fellow, he'd served in elite units of the IDF. Suddenly, he'd become a broken vessel.

I took care of everything he needed and stayed by his side. I explained to him that he had a good chance of recovering fully and returning to his regular activities. I told him story after story about people who'd gone through the same thing and who now showed no signs of their injuries. For obvious reasons, I left out the stories with less optimistic outcomes.

He barely communicated with me. My heart told me that aside from the injury, something else was going on, but I couldn't figure out what.

I extended my stay. When the time came, I got the airline to arrange special seating to accommodate the wounded man on a flight back to Israel. It wasn't cheap. The family paid some of the expenses, and others, including me, did the rest. The wounded man was transferred to Israel for further treatment and rehabilitation. The African hospital, though surprisingly professional, was still a hospital in a third-world country.

At the airport back in Israel, I met the man's father, who was then in his sixties. He looked like the nonreligious kibbutznik he was, but he was surprisingly full of warmth and love toward me, an obviously *frum* man. He thanked me warmly for all I had done for his son.

We parted ways, but not completely. Every so often I'd call to see how things were going. Rehabilitation was taking time, in part because the breaks were complex. There seemed to be another reason the process was prolonged, a hidden reason that I had sensed even in Africa, but I had no idea what it was.

One day when I called to ask the father about his son's progress, I told him that I felt something more than just broken bones was bothering him.

"You have no idea how right you are!" He asked me to meet him without his son's knowledge.

We met in my office. He kept thanking me until I was forced to tell him to stop. It took him a few moments to gather his thoughts, and then he began.

"Do you see my hand?" he said. "The spirit of God is in this hand."

I won't tell you what went through my mind at that moment. Let me just say it was along the lines of, *He needs to be hospitalized, the sooner the better.* But I said nothing.

"I sound crazy, don't I?" the bareheaded man said. "But once you hear my story, you'll understand.

"I was only a boy when the Nazis invaded Hungary. I suffered all the hardships along with my parents. I remember my parents whispering terrible things they'd heard, rumors about what was happening to the Jews of Europe. But no one believed that such things could take place.

"By 1944, it was clear that the situation was bad. Many people had been forced on transports and their fate was unknown. The rumors turned out to be true, yet people still couldn't grasp what that meant.

"One day, my father told me that we were going to say good-bye to the Belzer Rebbe, who was leaving by train for Eretz Yisrael. I was only nine years old when I walked with my father to the train station in Budapest to see the Rebbe. We were crushed by the crowd. My father was a strong man, and he carried me on his shoulders and pushed his way forward right up to the train. The train windows were very high up, and my head reached to the level of the people inside. My father told me, 'When you see the Belzer Rebbe, ask him for a blessing.' He stayed close to the train and began walking alongside the cars. He asked me at every window if I saw the Rebbe, and each time I said no.

"Then my father paused for a moment, to regain his strength. Just then, I saw the Rebbe right in front of me. I was so startled that I didn't even tell my father. I found myself looking into the Rebbe's face. He smiled at me and then reached out through the window to take my hand. 'May you grow up and bring *asach asach Yiddishe nachas* (a great deal of Jewish *nachas*).'

"My father wasn't aware of any of this. He started walking alongside the train, and then I remembered to shout at him, 'I got a blessing from the Rebbe and he held my hand!' At first my father didn't believe me, but then he turned around and got a glimpse of the Rebbe. He moved away from the train, lowered me from his shoulders, hugged me, and said, 'The spirit of God is in your hand.'

"We went home. I heard him repeat that sentence to me and others with glowing eyes many times. 'The spirit of God is in his hand.' Not that he had a lot of time to say it. Only two months later they dragged us to the train that took us to Auschwitz. There I was separated from my father and mother. Several hours later, I was told that the smoke I saw was their bodies burning.

"Somehow I survived until the end of the war. I made aliya to Israel and was sent to a kibbutz. I did not remain religious, because there was no one to teach me and because, like many of my fellow survivors, I was very angry about what had happened. I know that many came out of it with their faith even stronger, but I wasn't one of them.

"I grew up and got married. My wife and I have a son and a daughter. My son grew up and entered the army, where he joined an elite commando unit. He was promoted to officer and eventually reached lieutenant colonel. I looked forward to the day he would marry, but he was busy up to his neck in the army and never found the time for it.

"When he turned thirty-five, he retired from the army and started earning money in Africa training armies and police forces. The work brings in a lot of money, but it's very dangerous. My son was never one to back away from danger.

"After two years of this, he told me he was planning on getting married. 'Who's the girl?' I asked him. He told me he'd met someone there, an American computer expert. My first question was, 'Is she Jewish?'"

"'Come on, Abba. Really.'

"'Just tell me if she's Jewish.'

"'I didn't ask and it doesn't interest me,' my son said.

"'I know I never raised you to be religious,' I said to him, 'but staying Jewish is the minimum. At least find out.'

"'There's nothing to find out,' he said. 'She's Catholic. Her parents are devout Catholics, but they don't care if she marries a Jew and they're not asking me to convert.'

"It hit me like a ton of bricks. I started crying and begging him not to do something like that. He was furious. He said I had no right to tell him who to marry, especially not at his age and after the way I had raised him. I told him I wasn't telling him what to do, I was only asking. 'You don't even have the right to ask,' he said.

"I was devastated. With all that I'm nonreligious and don't keep a single mitzvah, not even Shabbat or keeping kosher, my Jewish identity has always been very important to me, maybe because of the Rebbe's blessing. I thought about the life I'd lived. I hadn't even fulfilled the Rebbe's blessing. If the spirit of God was in my hand, where was it?

"Several months passed, and then my son took a trip into the heart of the jungle. One afternoon as he watched monkeys hanging on a tree, he got it into his head to climb up and do the same thing. As he climbed, he stepped on a weak branch and fell to the ground from a height of a six-story building. That kind of a fall would kill most people, but not him. He survived with complex fractures of the pelvis, legs, and ribs. He was rushed to the hospital, and his intended went there with him.

"He was rushed into emergency surgery, and while she waited outside, the doctors explained the surgery her groom-to-be was undergoing. 'But why do you have to put in so many screws and plates?' she wanted to know.

" 'They hold the bone fragments together so they can heal,' the doctor answered.

" 'Wait a second – are those screws going to remain in his body?'

" 'Yes, of course. The bones will rejoin, but the screws will remain. To remove them, you'd have to break the bones again.'

"She waited there another half hour, and then gave the nurse a note to give my son when he woke up from the operation.

"When he came out of the anesthesia, the first thing he asked was where she was. The staff avoided giving him an answer. Only after he was transferred to the ward did the nurse give him the note.

"There was only one word written there: 'Sorry.'

"That's it. She just up and left. He tried to reach her but was told that she'd quit her job and left Africa. She didn't want to deal with a person whose body is full of screws.

"My son was broken twice – once from the fall, and once by her," the man said. "You're the first person to notice it, and that's why I told you the whole story."

We sat there in silence. I didn't know what to say.

"Look," he said, "I hate to ask you for a favor after all you've done, but maybe you know someone for my son? Believe me, he's a really great guy. He's walking normally now and has a new job at a good salary. But something inside him died. I'm sure that if you find him a good wife, he'll be a wonderful husband. Maybe I didn't raise him to be a good Jew – " his voice broke "but I did raise him to be a mensch."

I asked him to let me think about it, though the idea of me knowing someone for his son sounded farfetched. I'm no *shadchan*, and the world I live in is *frum*. Where would I find a girl for a nonreligious guy who almost married a Catholic?

✵ ✵ ✵

When I told my wife the story, her reaction was, "What about Anna?"

Anna is another story. I once flew in the private plane of a famous Russian oligarch, along with his wife and sixteen other passengers who were all there for the same purpose.

Our group wanted to pray on the plane, but there was a problem. A flight attendant kept walking around, and none of us wanted to ask her to give us our privacy for a while. It wasn't our plane, and we didn't know how she would react.

My wife volunteered for the job. She explained to the woman that the men needed to pray and asked if she would mind sitting down somewhere else until they finished.

The flight attendant was surprised, but she readily agreed. She and my wife went to sit near the kitchen, and they began to talk.

The flight attendant began by laughing and saying she wasn't used to people telling her to leave. Usually, she got the opposite request. My wife laughed with her, and then explained in detail what was going on. As they talked, my wife discovered that the flight attendant was a Jewish girl from Russia, highly educated, but who knew nothing about her religion. She didn't like working as a flight attendant and didn't especially enjoy the type of people she met on the job.

When I went back to my seat, my wife told me about the conversation. For some reason, I went over to the business magnate and asked him if he had a different job for the flight attendant. My wife had given her high praise for her grace and character. He talked to the girl and found out that she had graduated with honors in economics and business administration. He made a few calls, and then said, "Starting tomorrow, you'll be working in my Israeli office. Work hard, work well, and you can work your way up. Maybe someday you'll even manage the place for me."

From that favorable beginning, our relationship with Anna continued. Anna rose quickly through the ranks, and our home was hers. Occasionally she spent Shabbos with us. She wasn't religious, and we didn't pressure her to become religious, either. But we always told her that she was naturally *frum* in her modesty, her gentleness, and her outlook on life. She didn't respond, but just smiled and stayed as she was.

"Let's try to do something," my wife suggested after I'd told her the story. "They're both nonreligious, they're both in danger of assimilating. I think if they marry each other it will save them both from marrying out."

We invited him for a Shabbos. He accepted our invitation eagerly, either out of gratitude or because he didn't have anything better to do. We invited Anna too, and they talked. She took an interest in his army years and his new job, and he in her job. We didn't have to work too hard to create a connection between them.

They started dating, and within a few months, his father called, all excited. "My son is going to marry Jewish and it's all because of you!"

They got married, still not religious, but they kept up their connection with us. It's funny, but it was only after they got married that they warmed up to religion. She started first, but it didn't take much pushing on her part for him to join her. It had been inside her all this time, but her personality couldn't take drastic changes. She followed his more dominant personality, and they both began the process of *teshuvah*.

And they did it all the way. We couldn't believe our eyes, the way they changed and became religious and then *frum*. He grew a beard and peyos, she started covering her hair, they moved to a *frum* neighborhood, and they sent their children to the strongest *frum* schools. Eight children were born to this couple over the years, and except for people who knew their story, you'd never guess their past. They integrated beautifully.

I can't describe what happened to the father. I believe that if his son had gone this route in the usual way, he would have been furious. But his fear of losing his descendants to another nation made him happy and supportive – and brought even him a little bit closer to religion.

"The spirit of God is in my hand," he likes to say. "The Rebbe's blessing came true. I have *asach asach Yiddishe nachas.*"

21

The Exchange

I'm your average *kollel yungerman*, living in a community of like-minded people. About three years ago, my older brother, father of seven and also still in *kollel*, ran into serious trouble with his eldest son. The boy acted *chutzpadik* to his parents and teachers, and then stopped going to school. His behavior was way out of bounds. I started hearing from my brother that he couldn't take it anymore and that he was thinking of throwing the kid out of the house.

I told him he should consider his words and actions very carefully. He invited me to spend a day of my vacation in his house so I could see for myself how his son acted.

During the three-week summer break, I brought my whole family to visit. The scenes my wife and I witnessed were not at all what my brother had described. It wasn't the boy's behavior that bothered us, but his parents'. We couldn't stand the way they were treating him.

It seemed like they were both out to get him. They pounced on every word he uttered. They shut him up, put him down, dismissed whatever he said, and disparaged him. They criticized everything he did and everything he didn't do – or didn't do well enough to their liking.

My heart went out to the kid. Something had to be done about what was going on. I tried talking with my brother about it, but he wasn't open to hearing what I had to say.

"You don't know what this kid is doing to us," he said to me. "If you had to put up with what we do, you wouldn't be so quick to give me advice. Too bad I told you about it."

At the end of our visit, I offered to have the boy live with us. I told him I'd be able to get him enrolled in the local school and said I'd help him improve his behavior. The main goal of the move, though, would be to put an end to the confrontations.

My brother asked his wife what she thought, and they were both of one mind. I couldn't believe how fast they agreed to get rid of him.

Amazingly, the boy himself was just as ready to leave them as they were to have him go. He couldn't wait to leave the home he viewed as too strict, even though my own home, by any assessment, was a lot stricter. He packed and came back with us.

We got him enrolled locally, gave him a room in our house, and then waited to see what would happen.

The first thing I noticed was the boy's negative attitude toward doing mitzvos. If we didn't remind him to make a blessing before and after he ate, he wouldn't do it. If we didn't push him to daven, he wouldn't bother. However, unlike my brother, I had a lot of patience for the boy. I reminded him gently, without any feelings of anger or inner tension. After my reminder, he'd *bentch*. Though I had to remind him at almost every meal, I never found myself getting angry about it. I certainly never exploded – and not because I didn't care. It's just that I knew he was a kid with certain issues, and I was sure that anger and explosions would only be counterproductive.

During a conversation with my brother, I mentioned this. "Look how I treat him," I said. "I don't torture him, I don't hurt his feelings, and I certainly don't shout at him."

My brother made no reply. I regretted my criticism as soon as I ended the call. Why did I have to hurt his feelings? What good would it do?

❊   ❊   ❊

There were ups and downs, but basically the boy went to school every day, and more or less did what he was told – not because he wanted to, but because he'd been asked. It didn't bother me in the least.

He hit a rough patch when someone asked about his family and mentioned his little sister. That hurt. He cried and was sad for quite some time. My heart went out to him. I practically begged my brother to take him back home. But his wife wouldn't hear of it. She said it would be a shame to spoil things. The boy was doing well, as was the family. The other children were thriving. Without the stress of having him around, and without him setting a bad example, they were behaving beautifully. They said we should try not to remind him of his home so that he wouldn't think of it and want to go back.

To me, this seemed like the epitome of selfishness and cruelty. They were more interested in peace and quiet than in doing their duty as parents and tackling their parenting chal-lenge. I thought about the many parents who faced major problems, parents who fought the courts for the right to have their child live with them, and here they were fighting for their child *not* to live with them.

I was very critical of my brother and his wife, which made me treat their son with twice the love I would have given him otherwise.

❊   ❊   ❊

A year after my nephew came to live with us, one of our children started slacking off in school. It got worse. He began cutting class and getting in trouble with teachers. To make a long story short, he was exhibiting the same sort of behavior his cousin had.

Don't get me wrong. It wasn't due to his cousin's influence. It was a different sort of problem altogether.

My nephew was an average student. He performed as he should, went to school every day, and didn't cause any trouble. His problem was an inner, spiritual one, which we'd been able to mask. No one knew that he wasn't careful about *bentching*. When I reminded him, I did it by way of a private signal between the two of us, so that none of the other children would notice. As far as they were concerned, he was a great kid. He wasn't off the *derech* and didn't look like he was headed that way. His struggle was internal. He lacked enthusiasm in his *yiras Shamayim* – a subject that deserves a story of its own. There are kids like that.

But my son was on a real downward spiral. He was rebellious, scorning all those who sat and learned. He stopped going to daven, and he skipped school all the time. His behavior at home was atrocious.

What drove me up the wall the most was the truancy. I fought with him about it every single day, and it was a source of tremendous tension between us.

One day, after certain behavior of his that crossed all spiritual boundaries, I found myself telling his siblings to stay away from him. I was afraid they'd go off the *derech* because of him.

We went through a terrible time. We got caught up in an emotional and *chinuch* maelstrom with our son without stopping to think about what we were doing.

My brother became aware of it through his son, who had started to go home for an occasional Shabbos. My brother and his family came for a Shabbos, and he noticed my relationship with my son. Before he left for home, he took me aside and said,

"My guess is that you're probably too ashamed to admit it, but it looks to me like you've got the same problem I had."

I felt attacked. "You're right," I said smugly. "I have a problem, a bigger one than yours was. But I'm trying to deal with it. I'm not dumping my kid."

I could see he was hurt, but he didn't say anything.

I was locked in a fierce battle with my son. It reached the point where we employed some very harsh methods, like locking him in his room for hours if he acted out. I had reached the end of my rope.

One day, I lashed out at him. "You're killing your parents!" I screamed. I gave him a look that I thought expressed pain, but apparently he interpreted it as something much stronger.

He looked at me and said, "I know you hate me. I always said so, and now I see it's true."

I didn't deny it, both because I didn't have the energy to deal with him and…because I knew deep in my heart that he was right. My son was tormenting me. He was hurting me by talking and acting *chutzpadik* in every way possible. How did he get that way? What did I ever do to him for him to treat me like that?

As I thought about these things, it occurred to me that the battle between me and my son had become personal. My outbursts and attacks on him had nothing to do with *chinuch*. I was getting even with him on a personal level instead of parenting him. It suddenly occurred to me that maybe I should be treating him was the way I treated his cousin.

Why wasn't I?

The answer was crystal clear.

I called my brother and asked him to let my son stay with him for a while. He was taken aback. He couldn't understand why I had changed my mind.

"I thought I was a better parent than you are," I told him. "After all, I was able to treat your son in a sensible, healthy manner. I didn't hurt his feelings. I encouraged him to improve in a gentle manner, with love and by giving a positive personal example of the right way to act. And it worked. But now, with my own son, it's not working. I wasn't able to relate to him the way I relate to your son. Now I understand why many educators fail with their own children. I think it's because as a parent, you're not operating solely through intellect, but with a parent's love. I think that sometimes this emotion erases your understanding and knowledge of what's really the right thing to do."

We made up that he would take the boy for a trial period, and that's what happened.

So, my son moved into my brother's home and – surprise, surprise – my brother treated him just the way I'd treated his son.

Two years passed. Both boys changed, became more serious, and eventually each returned to his own home. The process we went through is too deep and complex to be put into words. I can only say that today my son and I have a deep connection. He respects me and tries to make me happy.

I think everyone should hear my story, especially because I think the solution wasn't ideal. I don't think parents should give up one of their children, even for a limited amount of time. The point is to proceed with caution in the parent-child dynamic, especially when your reactions seem to be a departure from true *chinuch*.

Also, I think that even master educators who know the inner workings of a child need to be very careful when it comes to their own children. Their expertise can mislead them into thinking they're interacting with their own children according to their intellectual understanding of the situation. They're not aware that another complex system is at work in the parent-child relationship: emotions. Without this awareness, inadvertently they can be hurt and hurt others and will find themselves acting and reacting in ways very different from their usual behavior.

The true way to educate is to educate – not to hurt, embarrass, hit, or persecute the child to death. When a person is objective toward the child, he knows exactly how to educate him. The minute it's not his own son, he's less afraid of how he'll turn out, which is exactly why he'll treat him with more restraint and greater wisdom. The minute it's his son, personal issues enter the picture and are likely to lead to different outcomes.

Rare is the person who can be completely objective toward his own children when they stray and act toward them as if they were someone else's children, with wisdom and objectivity. I heard about one of today's *gedolim* whose son didn't follow in his footsteps. Still, he maintained a close relationship with him, despite his own personal standing. He was able to separate his own feelings and interests from the issues at hand, like a master educator. His son loved and respected him for it.

I don't recommend doing what my brother and I did. Removing a child from his home is an extreme step to take. But it highlights an important fact: a person is too close to himself and his child to view the situation with the objectivity it needs. He has to realize that his buttons are being pushed – and to fight against his natural tendency to react.

Recently, I talked with my son, now a *yeshivah bachur* almost in *shidduchim*, about that time. He broke down and cried. The pain at being abandoned tore him apart. Both of us cried for having reached places like that. At the same time, we knew that if we hadn't done it, we wouldn't be as close as we are today. It was rough, but worth it.

22

In a Land Not Sown

I've disguised the identities of people and places in this story because it hasn't ended, and it's best that no one know the people involved.

It all began several years ago when a noted Torah figure decided to open a yeshivah far from the usual centers of learning here in Eretz Yisrael. Plans were quickly turned into action, and the *rav* and his assistant were soon on the road checking the options. Their driver took them from one *moshav* to the next, looking for the right place.

The *rav* met with one refusal after another.

After a long day of rejections, they were just about ready to give up when they passed our *moshav*. The driver asked if there was any point in entering our small, neglected *moshav*, and the *rav* said yes.

Pesach was only a few days away, and preparations were at a feverish pitch. Like most of the other homes on the *moshav* right then, ours was one huge mess.

The knocks on the door startled us. Equally surprising was the sight of a mini-delegation at our doorstep: the distinguished *rav* accompanied by his assistant and driver. He asked if he could come in and talk with us for a few minutes, seeing that ours was the home of Rabbi of the *moshav*.

It was an uncomfortable moment. We couldn't find a decent place to seat him. We invited him into another room that was less of a mess, but he wouldn't hear of it. He sat down in the nearest empty chair right next to the dining room table piled high with Pesach kitchenware and said, "We've come to open a yeshivah here."

Our jaws dropped. Our *moshav* was just about the last place in the world suited to opening a yeshivah. It was a completely nonreligious place, with only two *frum* families. Other communities in the area were either religious or nonreligious, but none of them had such adamantly antireligious members as ours. Did the *rav* really want to open a black-hat yeshivah here?

The *rav* asked if we had a shul or study hall that might serve the purpose, and our father had no choice but to take him to see the *moshav's beit knesset*. On the way there, my father told him that the *beit knesset* had been very run down until a year ago, at which time a family had paid to have it renovated, though no one knew why.

"Now we know why," the *rav* said as they arrived at the building. "This is exactly what we need. The yeshivah will be founded here."

Our father, the Rabbi of the *moshav*, didn't know how to respond. Such a decision needed the approval of the *moshav's* executive committee. Seeing the lights on in the *moshav's* offices across from our house, he went in and found out that a meeting of the executive committee was taking place that very minute. He suggested to the rav that they present his request right then and there.

They went in, and the *rav* presented his request. The committee members told the *rav* that they would need to bring it to a vote of the general assembly. Only a majority could decide for or against opening a yeshivah on the *moshav*.

This was just a ruse, of course. The *moshav*'s members had no intention of allowing a yeshivah to be established on their turf.

In the following days, one person's name came up repeatedly as the member most adamantly opposed to the idea: "Alex." Alex was a founding member, so his opinions carried a lot of weight. He talked to everyone, convincing, cajoling, and even coercing them to vote no.

Once the *rav* discovered what was behind the foot-dragging, he dispensed with seeking permission. Within weeks, a yeshivah filled with dozens of *bachurim* began the new *zman*, without any kind of vote or authorization from the *moshav*.

Now the members had a good excuse for their opposition to the yeshivah. "All of a sudden they come along and think they can put a yeshivah here without our permission!"

A handful of people supported the yeshivah and even helped get it started. A dining room was set up in an enclosure that used to be a goat pen. Its owner, a member of the *moshav*, sold his herd of goats and brought in a caravan with a kitchen that was roomy enough to serve as a dining room. The man himself served as the cook. The place had a small, old-fashioned refrigerator that wasn't big enough for the yeshivah. The yeshivah administration put up a notice on the bulletin board outside the *moshav*'s grocery that said, "Wanted: Used refrigerator."

The notice was ripped off the bulletin board within the hour.

Someone must have read it in that hour, though, because several days later, when the *bachurim* arrived in the morning they discovered a brand-new industrial-sized refrigerator parked outside the building. They assumed the yeshivah had bought it, but the yeshivah's administrator was just as surprised to see it as they were. He tried to find out who had ordered such an expensive new refrigerator, but met with a brick wall. No one had ordered the refrigerator. It had just landed on the yeshivah's doorstep in the middle of the night.

The refrigerator was put straight to work with the yeshivah no closer to knowing the identity of the mysterious donor. The best guess was that someone on the *moshav* had decided to donate it but was afraid of drawing the ire of the other members.

The yeshivah had no dorm, so the *bachurim* lived in homes rented from *moshav* members. They paid much more than the going rate in an old, neglected *moshav* such as ours.

Alex went from house to house warning members not to rent to the yeshivah. This drove up the price on units whose owners ignored him. Meanwhile, the yeshivah kept getting anonymous donations that covered the cost of the rentals. Two forces were at work, the force of evil headed by Alex, which worked behind the scenes, but whose actions leaked out somehow, and the force of good, which was completely hidden. No one knew who made sure the yeshivah was well taken care of – not even my father.

Whenever the *rav* who founded the yeshivah came to the *moshav* for a Shabbos, he and his *rebbetzin* stayed with us. He always gave a talk in shul on Shabbos, though some people stood up and walked out. In the best-case scenario, they didn't stand up as soon as he walked in; in the worst, they not only stood up but, sad to say, cursed him loudly before leaving.

But this was nothing compared to the tactics used by the yeshivah's most adamant opponent, Alex. No cursing for him; he wouldn't stoop so low. But what he did was far more dangerous – he went to the courts.

While the yeshivah's students, staff, and supporters were given the cold shoulder and threatened by their opponents, a legal battle raged between the *moshav* and the yeshivah, with the prime instigator being Alex. Not that his name appeared on any of the documents. You couldn't prove anything against him, because he worked behind the scenes. This made the threat more powerful – and more dangerous.

When the case reached the stage where it seemed obvious we would lose, one of the top lawyers in the country suddenly appeared out of nowhere saying he'd been hired to represent the yeshivah. He mentioned a name we didn't recognize. We tracked down this benefactor, who turned out to be a wealthy realtor. He told us he'd been sent by someone else to pay for legal representation for the yeshivah, but that he was not at liberty to divulge the person's name. He ended the conversation abruptly after telling us not to call him again.

The whole thing was strange beyond belief. Strong forces were at play, but we had no idea who was behind them.

Our first reaction was to refuse the services of this famous, expensive lawyer. We were afraid he'd been hired by our opponents to sabotage our case. On second thought, we reached the conclusion that we didn't have much to lose. It looked like we were set to lose anyway, so it didn't make sense that someone would have paid all that money to hire the services of an unnecessary attorney. Besides, this attorney was so big that he'd have no reason to take on a client just to lose the case.

We decided to go for it.

His presentation before the court was a stroke of genius that turned the case on its head in the eleventh hour. He unearthed the information that most of the factories on the *moshav* were operating without a license or permit of any kind. He also alluded in court to some illegal businesses in which the *moshav* was a partner. The *moshav* was caught in a legal tangle, with some of its members facing possible criminal charges.

Our opponents quickly withdrew charges, and the court gave the yeshivah a permit to remain. Our opponents were ordered to pay an astronomical amount of money to cover the yeshivah's legal costs, though said costs had been minimal.

❋ ❋ ❋

But the burning hatred remained. The enmity and anger
intensified until it reached a point where the *bachurim* walked in
pairs for protection against physical attacks by the more extreme
elements opposed to the yeshivah. More than once the police
were called in to break up such clashes.

Within a short time, the prime antagonists began to suffer
personal misfortune, whether in business, health, or other
areas. It seemed obvious that their woes were retribution for
the disgrace they had caused to the holy Torah and its scholars.
One person had a large herd of sheep that was stolen down to
the last lamb. Each sheep was worth thousands of shekels, so it
added up to a major loss. The second protester came to my father
one day trembling with fear. He said that Arabs were harassing
him. They accused him of stealing from them and threatened to
kill him. My father made use of the opportunity to say that he
should quickly beg forgiveness for the anguish he had caused
the *Rav* who established the yeshivah. The man went and did
as my father suggested. He apologized and promised never to
disparage the Torah and its scholars again. You might not believe
this, but the Arabs just disappeared. The same way they came,
they just went and left him alone. The man took it as a sign
and, at my father's suggestion, began putting on tefillin every
morning. He doesn't dare to talk or act against Torah and Torah
scholars till this very day.

Nothing happened to Alex. Someone pointed out that there
was a difference between him and the others, because when a
person speaks out against Hashem and His Torah publicly, the
retribution is given here in this world in public, unlike someone
who does so secretly. It's not that he's absolved. It's just that
there's an element here of measure for measure.

❋ ❋ ❋

Recently the yeshivah approached the *moshav*'s directorate with a surprising offer: to construct a building for the yeshivah in exchange for a hefty payment to the *moshav*. But the hatred for Torah overpowered the financial temptation, though the *moshav* was drowning in debt.

Again they decided to hold a general meeting of all members. Naturally, the decision was not to allow the yeshivah to build, due largely to concerted efforts made to bring in votes (as long as they were against) from registered members who no longer lived on the *moshav* but still had the right to vote. At the meeting it was decided that the yeshivah should leave the *moshav*.

Decisions are one thing, reality another. The yeshivah is still here, alive and well, filled with outstanding *bachurim*.

❈ ❈ ❈

One day, one of the yeshivah's opponents strode into the *beis midrash* in the middle of *seder*, stood next to the *bimah*, and began to lecture the *bachurim*. He told them that God didn't want them to be there on the *moshav*, that it was a *chillul Hashem*, totally inappropriate, and no good.

The *bachurim* were instructed to keep their heads down and their eyes on the Gemara, and to continue learning. And that's exactly what they did, their voices rising with renewed enthusiasm.

In yet another attempt to lower the morale of the *bachurim*, the opponents asked a few secular girls to hang around inside the yeshivah and talk to the boys. They even threatened to open a pool on the grassy area outside the yeshivah, and to blare music on Shabbos afternoon. When they saw that all this didn't help and that no one even blinked, they ratcheted up the level of threats.

One morning, the *bachurim* encountered a pile of new furniture outside the yeshivah: *shtenders* and chairs for the *beis midrash*; bookshelves and closets for the *beis midrash* and their rooms; large air conditioners to replace the yeshivah's broken ones; plus much more, all new.

The yeshivah's manager estimated that the gift was worth about 100,000 shekels. Obviously, the same person who had bought the refrigerator and paid for the lawyer had come through for the yeshivah once again.

But with all the good, there were some bad moments as well. One day, one of the *rabbanim* set out on trip with his family. A few miles out of the *moshav*, they encountered a black car blocking the road. They were forced to stop, and ordered to open all the windows. Faced with no real choice, they complied. They then were treated to a barrage of shouts, curses, spitting, and hair-raising threats.

These opponents were young and new to the *moshav*. They didn't yet know that Hashem runs the world. Shortly after the incident, the police caught them. One of them was no less than a security officer of the *moshav*! He lost his job because he'd shown he wasn't worthy of it. Not only that, but his weapon was taken away from him because someone who abuses his position might also come to abuse his weapon.

We found out that only a few months earlier this man had been a high-ranking police officer who was caught breaking the law. He'd been dismissed and had taken this new job overseeing security on the *moshav*. Now, due to his foolish conduct, he'd lost his second chance and the opportunities it might have led to.

At the end of Tishrei, one of the *moshav*'s members donated a new *sefer Torah* to the *beit knesset*. A few people on the *moshav* left their homes to participate, but as you might suspect, most of the celebrants came from the outside. *Frum* Yidden from all over the country but primarily from settlements in the south, gave expression to their love of Torah, dancing joyously as they escorted the *sefer Torah* to its new home.

The yeshivah continues to grow. *Bachurim* sit learning day and night. The yeshivah's opponents are also busy, each with his own trouble. As I mentioned earlier, one lost his job, another fell ill, a third was slapped with a defamation lawsuit brought by the yeshivah, and others had troubles as well.

✤   ✤   ✤

The story is still going on, but one person who'd been hidden from us, recently became known.

One day the *bachurim* found a new generator next to the building. It was worth a lot of money, and bringing it there must have taken a semitrailer.

This time, though, the yeshivah's administrator didn't need to investigate.

Two weeks before, due to repeated vandalism, the yeshivah had installed security cameras. All he had to do now was to watch.

At first, he saw what he'd expected to see. A truck pulled up to the yeshivah, Arab workers carefully lowered the generator, then got back in the truck and drove off.

He decided to replay the segment. This time he noticed that the workers looked in a certain direction, as if listening to orders. He played the video from the second camera and suddenly saw the figure who gave the orders.

The man was covered by a parka, but for one brief moment the hood fell back to reveal his face.

Alex.

We were stunned. And confused. We had no idea why the leader of the opposition would help us, and to such an extent. Could it be that he was the mystery man who had paid double: to sue us and to pay for our defense?

It was decided not to probe the matter. Maybe one day the mystery would be solved. Meanwhile, we continued to be the grateful beneficiaries of the gifts, as well as the blows, from Heaven. Now we understand better the *mishnah* that says a person should make a blessing on the bad just like he does on the good.

The *rav* who founded the yeshivah with such dedication is no longer in this world, but his memory lives on. The yeshivah he established is still is a beacon of light, and the credit remains his for generations to come, until the end of time.

23

Money Laundering

With all the arguments and fights going on, the story I'm about to tell you is like a breath of fresh air or ice-cold water on a hot summer's day, or any other expression you want to use.

I'll start by telling you what I do for a living. I'm an electrician, but it's hard to call me just an electrician. I work with anything related to electricity, which means that over and above replacing blown fuses, installing new outlets and switches, and repairing electrical appliances, I'm sort of like a bank of replacement parts for refrigerators, washers, dryers, and dishwashers.

When *you* see an abandoned washing machine, you don't give it a second glance. But *I see* it as a potentially valuable collection of dozens of still-working parts, from gaskets to a stainless steel drum, motor, screws, doors, hoses, and whatever.

When I see an abandoned electrical appliance, my automatic response is to load it into my van. It doesn't matter if I'm on my way to a wedding or coming home from a PTA meeting. For me, electrical appliances – from irons to commercial freezers – are a source of income.

I load the appliance onto my van and bring it to my warehouse to inspect. If it can be repaired, you can make a thousand shekel or more on it. If it can't, then you start to take it apart until you can't tell what it was to begin with. Then you might make even more money off it, because next month one person might need a gasket, the second, a door, the third, a hose, the fourth, the drum, and each one will pay you between two hundred and four hundred shekels. That's how we earn a living.

When I say we, I mean me and my partner. We've been partners for the past twenty years. Both of us learn during the day, he in the morning, and me at night. I start work in the morning, and in the afternoon we work together. We do some of the work together, and some we do on our own. We share equally what we earn when we work together, and *baruch Hashem*, it's a good income.

❀   ❀   ❀

One day, my partner called me at eleven in the morning. "I need you here right away," he said.

"What's up?"

"You'll see when you get here."

"Can it wait?" I asked him.

"It's the last thing in the world that can wait," he said.

I started imagining all kinds of things he could have found, like maybe an oven worth two thousand shekels, for instance. There are people, believe it or not, who will throw out a working oven instead of cleaning it. Or maybe he'd found an commercial refrigerator worth five thousand shekels.

When I reached the address he gave me, I saw him leaning against an old, rusty dryer whose door was about to fall off. In seconds, my professional assessment told me that we'd be lucky to get even thirty shekels from this piece of junk.

"You brought me here for this washtub?" I asked him.

Then I noticed that he was sweating profusely. "What happened?" I asked him.

"Let's first get this thing in your van and then we'll talk."

We loaded up and headed out for the warehouse. We unloaded it, and only after he slammed the warehouse door closed did he bend down, reach into the piece of junk and pull out...an Elite coffee tin.

"Great," I said to him. "We made forty-nine shekels and ninety-nine agorot."

"Open it and you'll see we're talking about a little more than that," he said.

I opened the tin and saw that it was filled with two-hundred-shekel bills rolled up tightly.

"It was inside the machine, outside the drum," he told me.

We emptied the coffee tin. Who would have thought so much money could fit into such a small container? There were twenty-six wads, each with ten red bills tightly rolled and held by a rubber band. All together, it came to fifty-two thousand shekels.

"What now?" I asked him.

"We have to find out who threw this dryer away," he said.

We started our search. We put up notices on every nearby building asking who had recently discarded an old dryer. We wrote that an item had been found inside the dryer, but we didn't say what. With plenty of identifying signs that only we knew about, we weren't afraid of someone making a false claim.

Three days later, a woman in the neighborhood called me and said that she'd thrown out a dryer, but that she wasn't aware of losing anything.

"Did you buy the dryer in a store?" I asked her.

"No," she said. "I got it for nearly nothing six months ago from an electrician who deals in used appliances." She laughed. "And it was worth nearly nothing."

"Do you remember the name of the electrician?"

"Sure," she said, and told me his name.

We knew him. This branch of electronics is fairly small. There's a lot of competition, but at the same time, a feeling of camaraderie among us. He could call me and ask for a certain gasket, and I could call him and say, "Do you have a door for an old Electra?" Stuff like that.

I called him. "Did you sell a dryer to Mrs. So-and-so?" I asked him.

He started to stammer. "Leave me alone. I sold it to her for one hundred shekels. I told her it was without a guarantee. It worked for six months. That's four months longer than I thought it would last."

"Forget it," I said to him. "I have no complaints. I just want to find out who you got it from."

"What for?"

"No special reason," I said. "I just need to know. Do you know or not?"

"Nope," he said. "I found it someplace up north out in the open. I was on a trip with my kids. Instead of having fun, they had to help me drag that piece of junk into the car and then sit squashed together on the way back because it took up so much room. It's not leaving me alone, that dryer, even a year later. What's the story now?"

"Okay. If you say you didn't give it a guarantee, then I'll explain it to her." I changed the subject and ended the conversation.

Now we went to a *rav*.

It was clear that the woman had not put the money inside the dryer. Neither had the electrician. But we were still worried that maybe according to halachah the lost item belonged to one of them.

The *rav* said that since the money was not theirs, and from their answers they had no knowledge of its existence, they never acquired the money and it had no connection to them.

We asked what more we should do. He said that since the owner had probably given up all hope of ever seeing that money again, we could use it, on one condition. If, in the end of days, it turned out that the owner had not given up hope of getting the money back, because it had identifiable signs (the coffee tin, the rubber bands, the equal amount in the rolls), then we would have to return the money.

We left the *rav* and I said to my partner, "I'm so happy for you. You'll probably find a lot of good uses for fifty-two thousand shekels."

"You mean twenty-six thousand," he said.

"Why twenty-six?" I said to him. "We counted it together. It was fifty-two."

"Right," he said to me. "There was fifty-two, but we're partners, aren't we? I found some money and I need to share it with you."

I stopped walking. I looked at him and saw that he wasn't laughing. It took me a while to realize he meant every word.

"Are you crazy?" I said. "Maybe I'll be your partner if you win the lottery too."

"No," he said. "The lottery isn't connected to you, but the dryer is, 100 percent. It's part of our business together."

We started arguing about it. It got pretty heated. But he wouldn't give in. "You are going to take twenty-six thousand and not a cent less. There's nothing to discuss."

He pocketed half the money and put the other half on a stone wall nearby, got on his motorcycle, and rode off, leaving me there with the money.

❋   ❋   ❋

I went home and decided that I'd save the money.

The next day, someone asked me for a loan. I gave him the money, and I knew it was in good hands. That's how it went over the years. The money was returned and lent out several times, and then my partner's daughter got engaged. The *chasan* was a *ben Torah*, and I knew my partner had committed to quite a bit of money.

About three weeks before the wedding, my wife and I went to his house. We told them that we wanted to give them our present before the wedding so that they could use it during this crucial time.

We sat with them for a few minutes, and then we left to return home. We hadn't driven more than a few minutes when my cell phone rang.

"What's this supposed to be?" my friend asked.

"I saved the money that belongs to you," I told him. "It belonged to you to begin with, and I just kept it as a deposit."

"But there was only twenty-six thousand shekels. How did that suddenly grow to eighty thousand?"

"That's from a different reckoning," I told him. "You start work in the afternoon, and I work two hours in the morning. Ever since finding the lost item, I took it upon myself that from every job I did in the morning, you'd get half the payment, and this is the amount that accumulated from those two hours of work over the past two years."

That's the story. For quite a while, people have been telling me I should send it in to you. I didn't want to because I didn't see anything special about it. But then I started hearing about all kinds of arguments and disputes. I figured it might inspire people to read about a different kind of quarrel between two partners. It might give them food for thought. At the least, it will let them know there's a different way to handle things.

Author's note: I would like to express my appreciation to Mr. Y. B. for agreeing to have his story published.

24

You Can't Take It with You

Not long ago, Mr. Walder, I was walking through the streets of Meah Shearim with a guest from abroad. He wanted to buy presents to take back to his family, so we took advantage of our short tour to step into several stores.

This was in the morning. Suddenly, someone entered the store we were in and shouted, *"Shkiya! Shkiya!"* The owner of the store quickly told everyone that he had to close the store for a few minutes. Several customers protested, but he just pushed them out and disappeared.

My guest was astonished. *Shkiya* at 11:00 a.m.? What was going on?

I reassured him that sunset would take place that day at its regular time. The man had come to warn the storekeeper about someone. You'll excuse me, but I don't want to spell out here who the man was warning him against.

This incident, though, reminded me of a visit I made some thirty-five years ago to one of the government offices that no one wants to get summoned to and that no one ever goes to voluntarily.

But I did both things. I went there, and it was of my own free will.

Every time I go to interesting places, I take my wife along with me, both so that she can share my experiences and journeys, and also as my cover story, should the need arise. So this time too, I said to my wife, "Hurry. We're going to the Israel Tax Authority."

When my wife heard the words "tax authority," she almost fainted. She decided to put off fainting until she first heard from me what my business was with the tax people.

If there's one thing you should know, it's that people in Meah Shearim don't exactly have the most favorable view of having any direct contact (or even indirect contact) with government offices. But this particular government office draws the most criticism. Naturally, my wife narrowed her eyes at my double transgression, which would be looked at doubly unfavorably by our neighborhood's residents.

However, I explained to her that the purpose of my going to this particular government office, which is in charge of income tax, does not stem from curiosity or any desire to form a connection with the Zionists. I was going solely to give testimony in the case of CPA Reinitz, who's been our neighborhood accountant for as long as I can remember.

"What do you have against Reinitz?" my wife asked. "Why are you going to testify against him, especially now, when he's in trouble with the government over the Schlechter affair?"

"I don't have a single thing against Reinitz," I told her. "And if I did have anything against Reinitz, would it even occur to me to snitch on him to the tax authorities or any other government authorities?"

My wife chewed that over and decided to go with me to the lion's den. We flagged down a taxi and got in.

"The tax authority," I said to the driver.

"Wait a minute, mister!" the driver exclaimed. "You didn't even sit down and I didn't even start the meter. You can't bring a complaint against me when I didn't do anything."

I said to him, "Why do you suspect that I work for the tax authority? I only want to go there. And besides, don't turn on the meter, because I want to set a flat price of thirty shekels."

It took a while for the driver to start breathing normally. He shot us another suspicious glance, and just to be on the safe side, turned on the meter.

You see, there's a certain power to the words "tax authority" that works wonders. In my close to one hundred years, I've never seen a taxi driver turn on the meter of his own volition without the passenger using force, yet suddenly, when I said those two words, the man was reaching out his hand through the cobwebs to touch it.

❈   ❈   ❈

Before I tell you about the meeting, I need to point out a few things about Reinitz's office.

First of all, erase from your mind everything you've always imagined about an accountant's office before you even think of Reinitz. Reinitz's office is nothing more than a hole in the wall under some *mikveh*. When you get there, you'll be stepping on papers on which are listed the entire incomes of all the neighborhood's residents. The place is filled with people coming and going, smoking and eating and shouting at each other. Not Reinitz, though.

Actually, there's more than one Reinitz. There are a few of them, ranging in age from sixteen to ninety-six, all relatives that Reinitz employs in his business. But the main Reinitz is sixty-eight, and he's the boss of the entire Reinitz clan that is busy with accounting, secretarial work, janitorial services, manning the phones, and running errands.

Here, only Yiddish is spoken, and you can talk freely about all your dealings on condition that you talk in Yiddish and that you take the advice of the main Reinitz or one of his two assistants.

Reinitz carries a burning grudge against government offices, and he believes that paying even one single cent more than necessary is immoral. No one knows where he learned to be an accountant. Some say in Galicia, but you can be certain that no matter what happens to him, he'll get you off the hook. Not only that, but most times you'll also get a letter of apology, black on white, from the tax authority.

Reinitz always looks worried, but he never loses his calm, except in cases where the client who declared huge losses suddenly buys himself a luxury car. Then you can hear Reinitz shout from one end of the world to the other, and in many instances, he'll kick the fellow out of his office along with all his files. There's nothing Reinitz hates more than fools who turn themselves in to the government with their own two hands. More than once I've been asked to beg Reinitz to take back someone like this that he's thrown out of his office.

Now you'll understand why all of Meah Shearim and the whole Jewish world was astounded when Reinitz himself was called down to the tax authority and indicted over the disappearance of five million shekels from the estate of Levy Yitzchak Schlechter, z"l.

No matter which way you look at it, it came as a heavy blow to Reinitz. And don't think for a minute that the blow was to Reinitz's good name, because not a single person in Meah Shearim believed for a second that Reinitz had taken even a shekel of the deceased Schlechter's money. Reinitz didn't have a problem in Meah Shearim. His problem was with the tax authorities, who accused him of tax evasion on behalf of the departed Schlechter.

When I met Reinitz in Zupnik, he looked like he was under a lot of pressure. But that was nothing new, because, as I said, he always looked worried. However, unlike all other times, this time Reinitz really was worried and didn't just look it. After talking with him for a few minutes, I suddenly suggested, "Maybe I should go to the tax authority and testify on your behalf?"

Reinitz stared at me. "Are you trying to tell me that you're ready to enter the lion's den?"

"I want to tell you that for an elderly person my age, the tax authority reminds me more of a kitten's basket than a lion's den," I said to him. "In any case, all I need to do is tell them the story and that will be the end of it."

Reinitz showered me with blessings, but I said to him, "Don't shower me with anything. Just promise me that you'll take back Leitner, who you threw out for including gold faucets in his renovations. Don't get me wrong. I'm also against gold faucets, for reasons of modesty and good taste, but Leitner's tears of regret rival the water that comes out of his gold faucets."

"Consider Leitner back," Reinitz said. "Just go there and help me get rid of them."

The taxi driver arrived at the building. The meter said twenty-six shekels, but I gave him thirty because that was what we had agreed to.

❋   ❋   ❋

At the gate, I was asked where I was headed, to which I said, "Investigations." We went up to the second floor, where I told the guard that I had come to give testimony in the Reinitz case.

Within seconds, a crowd gathered around me. A few investigators rushed over to me and offered me water, tea, and coffee, and suggested that my wife wait in the meantime until I finished giving testimony. But I said, "With my wife, or nothing." They were burning up with curiosity to hear what I had to say, so they were willing to break the rules of protocol.

They took me into a room, and I started to tell them the whole story.

"It's not nice to speak about the dead," I began, "but here it's an urgent matter on which many Torah institutions depend, and therefore I allow myself to speak."

I then told the investigators the story of Levy Yitzchak Schlechter. I'm sorry, Mr. Walder, for resorting to a ruse here, but I'm making up a name because I don't want to hurt in any way the family of the person under discussion. Forgive me, and thanks for trusting me.

Levy Yitzchak Schlechter was one of the biggest tightwads in Meah Shearim, and some say in all of Yerushalayim.

I don't want to go into everything people say about Yerushalmi cheapskates, because people who've never known poverty and want or suffered hardship shouldn't talk. But if we choose to believe those slanderers, then Schlechter without a doubt beats all the other tightwads hands down.

Besides all the usual stuff like bumming cigarettes and eating meals regularly at whatever bris, bar mitzvah, and wedding he could find, Levy Schlechter knew how to make money.

But he didn't know how to spend it.

When I say "spend," I'm not talking about making donations or even spending on his family. I'm talking about expenses, such as, for instance, building a building. You need to pay for the cement, for shipping the goods. These are not things that you "give," but things for which you *owe payment*. And in this area, Schlechter was an expert.

To begin with, it was always hard to find Schlechter when he owed money. Schlechter didn't own a cell phone, and he had a special knack for not being in places where it didn't pay for him to be. Second, Schlechter had thousands ways of avoiding payment. Some of his famous lines were: "I have to order new checkbooks," "the bank is closed," "come back in another two weeks," "I'm out of the country," and "money is tight right now."

By the time a poor guy went through all seven levels of Gehinnom to find Schlechter, drag him to the bank, and make sure he had his checkbook with him, he faced the next obstacle in the war of attrition: the checks themselves.

Schlechter had a tendency to make mistakes when writing his checks, and though he wasn't strict with himself when it came to such mistakes, he demanded that the bank be very strict about them. Which means that the bank clerk knew full well that if he let a check go through on which Schlechter had retraced the number 3 to make it darker, he'd be taken to task for approving a check on which it was written not to allow any changes.

Similarly, Schlechter would forget to sign. People forget. What can you do? Sometimes Schlechter would sign, but forget to use the regular signature approved by the bank. Sometimes he'd sign twice, and sometimes he'd make a change and initial it. As a result, the bank would bounce the check for "technical" reasons. To get a replacement check out of him you'd have to go through the whole rigmarole from the very beginning.

Even after you got a kosher check, you had to watch out to make sure you didn't miss the deposit date. Among the avalanche of instructions Schlechter made sure to put on his checks was the following: "The check is valid for fifteen days from the date written."

If someone did manage to traverse this long route and get a check out of Schlechter that didn't have an erasure and that had a valid signature and everything else, he deserved a reward. Therefore, as opposed to his usual policy, Schlechter would not give a postdated check for another three months hence. No, he'd write a backdated check for fifteen days earlier and then give the check on a Friday. The poor man would make it to the bank on Sunday only to discover that he'd deposited the check too late… and everything went back to the beginning.

By now, the investigators were slightly amused by my story, even though I didn't understand what they found so funny about these kinds of tricks.

❋ ❋ ❋

It goes without saying that lots of income over the years with very few expenditures created a very positive balance in Schlechter's favor, but this balance made no difference when it came to his family. Actually, the richer Schlechter became, the lower his family's standard of living dropped, until it hit rock bottom. And no one could do a thing about it.

The only person who was able to help the family even a little was Reinitz. The accountant would sit and persuade Schlechter that if he didn't give his family a certain amount of money, they would go straight to the income tax authorities. And if there was anything Schlechter hated more than *spending* money it was *losing* it to income tax people. So this argument was the only thing that could squeeze some money out of him for his family.

The investigators facing me squirmed uncomfortably, but it didn't look like they were surprised by the unfriendly attitude expressed toward them by Schlechter or anyone else alive.

Anyway, Schlechter's family lived like that for years, in abject poverty, getting small crumbs thanks to Reinitz, and then Schlechter did the most generous thing he'd ever done in his life: he died.

The investigators started to laugh.

"Why are you laughing?" my wife cried out to them. "He really did die, Schlechter. What's so funny about that?"

But for some strange reason my wife's protests made them laugh even harder.

When his will was read, what do you think was discovered if not this short statement: "I order you to bury me along with all my wealth, except for immovable real estate. I appoint CPA Reinitz as my executor. Signed…"

Never was a nastier will written. On second thought, there probably was.

The investigators exchanged looks and confirmed with a nod that they too had not encountered a will as mean-spirited as that, though one of them remembered a fellow who'd left his entire estate to a dog. An argument began about which was worse, but in the end they agreed with me that leaving everything to a dog wasn't as bad as taking it to the grave where it could have no use, which put Schlechter back at the top of the pyramid.

The only person who saw the will was Reinitz. Under no circumstances did he dare tell the family about the sick plan of their beloved, if you can call him that. He concluded that there was no sense in fulfilling a will like that, which indicated that its writer was not in full possession of his faculties.

But Reinitz is and has always been straight as a ruler, and he would never dream of hiding a will entrusted to him.

And then he had an idea.

He had a few of Schlechter's signed checks in his possession, which he kept in his safe. He took one of those checks, made it out for five million shekels, and carefully recorded it in his records. At the funeral, he asked for a few minutes alone with the deceased. While everyone was wondering what special relationship he had with the departed, he snuck the check under the shrouds.

Since Reinitz suspected that Schlechter had told someone else besides him about the will, he dated the check for fifteen days earlier, and, after everyone left the cemetery, just to make sure, he stayed near the grave until the banks closed.

Then he went home knowing that he had fulfilled Schlechter's last will and testament while at the same time arranging for the family to receive a fortune that would sustain them till the end of their days, without them knowing a thing about the danger that had threatened their inheritance.

"You may be surprised to hear this," I told the investigators, "but Schlechter has made no attempt to cash the check."

The investigators burst out laughing.

"Ah, now you're laughing? But what you did to Reinitz is no joke, because a month later, you came and claimed that Reinitz had recorded a withdrawal of five million shekels from Schlechter's account. Since there was no activity in that account, you slapped him with a serious indictment for making a false declaration. The truth is that according to the law, the minute the check was made out it became a legal withdrawal in every way, even if the person decided not to cash it or a Higher Power prevented him from doing so. Furthermore, the government takes a big chunk out of the inheritance, and you still have complaints, eh?" I said to the astonished investigators sitting across the desk from me.

❋   ❋   ❋

They stood up, shook my hand, and said, "Relax. Go back to Meah Shearim and tell Reinitz that we're closing the case against him. Not only that, from today on, he's got an open door here due to all the good things you told us about him."

We stood up and left, but before we got out the door, my wife felt compelled to say something. As usual.

"An open door, huh? As if Reinitz would enjoy coming here," she said, then added, "What's so funny about what I said?"

We left the tax authority building and got into the taxi. "Meah Shearim," I said.

The driver looked at me and then looked suspiciously at the tax authority building. I watched as his hand reached for the meter.

"Without a meter," my wife shouted. "They've caused us enough trouble, those tax people. We lost four shekels on the way here." You've got to understand, Mr. Walder, that when all is said and done, my wife is a Yerushalmi whose family goes way back. Didn't you figure that out yet?

Glossary

The following glossary provides a partial explanation of some of the Hebrew, Yiddish (Y.), and Aramaic (A.) words and phrases used in this book. The spellings and explanations reflect the way the specific word is used herein. Often, there are alternate spellings and meanings for the words.

A"H: acronym for "*aleha hashalom*," peace unto her, added to the name of the deceased.

ASKAN (pl. ASKANIM): a community worker; a public activist.

AVREICH (pl. AVREICHIM): a young married Torah student.

AYIN HARA: the evil eye.

BA'AL TESHUVAH (pl. BA'ALEI TESHUVAH): a formerly nonobservant Jew who has returned to Jewish tradition and practice. Also, anyone who repents for behavior not sanctioned by the Torah.

BACHUR (pl. BACHURIM): a young man; a yeshivah student.

BADCHAN: (Y.) one who brings joy to wedding participants by reciting rhyming verses filled with wit and wisdom about the newly married couple and their families.

BARUCH HASHEM: "Thank God!"

BEIS DIN: a rabbinical court of law.

BEIS HAMIKDASH: the Holy Temple in Jerusalem.

BEIS MIDRASH: the study hall of a yeshivah.

BEIT KNESSET: a synagogue, a shul.

BENTCH: (Y.) to recite the grace after meals.

BIMAH: the reader's desk in the synagogue on which the Torah scroll is opened and read.

BITUL TORAH: neglect of Torah study.

BLI AYIN HARA: lit., "may there be no evil eye," an expression meant to ward off possible misfortune.

CHALAV YISRAEL: milk supervised by a Jew from the time of milking.

CHAREIDI (pl. **CHAREIDIM**): an ultra-Orthodox Jew.

CHASAN: a bridegroom.

CHEVRA: (A.) a group of friends.

CHILLUL HASHEM: desecration of God's Name.

CHINUCH: Jewish education and upbringing.

CHUPPAH: a wedding canopy; a wedding ceremony.

CHUTZPAH: insolence.

DAAS TORAH: the Torah outlook as stated by an outstanding Torah sage.

DERECH: lit., "path" (off the derech: off the path, i.e., no longer religious).

DERECH ERETZ: proper conduct.

DIVREI TORAH: words of Torah.

EMUNAS CHACHAMIM: staunch faith in Rabbinic leaders.

FRUM: (Y.) religious.

GABBAI: a synagogue officer.

GADOL HADOR: the leading Torah authority of the generation.

GEDOLIM (pl.): lit., "greats"; Torah leaders.

GEMACH: acronym for "gemilas chassadim"; a place where money or items are lent free of charge.

GESHMAK: (Y.) pleasure.

GLATT KOSHER: strictly kosher.

HASHEM: God.

HECHSHER: kashrus certification.

ILUI: a genius.

KALLAH: a bride.

KASHE: a difficult question in learning.

KEDOSHIM: holy martyrs of the Holocaust.

KESUBAH: a marriage contract.

KEVOD HARAV: lit., "Honored Rabbi"; a respectful form of address used when speaking to a distinguished Torah leader.

KIDDUSH HASHEM: sanctification of God's Name.

KIPPAH: a skullcap.

KIRUV: bringing nonreligious Jews back to their heritage.

KOLLEL: a center for advanced Torah study for adult students.

KOSEL: the Western Wall.

LEHIBADEL BEIN CHAIM: "May he be separated [from the aforementioned deceased] for life."

LIMUD, talk in *limud*: Torah learning; to speak in learning.

MA'ASER: tithe.

MASHGIACH: a spiritual guide in a yeshivah.

MASMID: a diligent yeshivah student.

MIDDOS: character traits.

MIKVEH: a pool for ritual immersion.

MOSHAV: a small, usually rural, Israeli settlement.

NACHAS: pride; satisfaction; pleasure.

NEIAS: (Y.) news.

NU: (Y.) "Well?" or "So?"

PARSHA: lit., "chapter" (in the *parsha*: in the chapter [about looking for a mate], i.e., looking to get married).

POSEK: a rabbi qualified to deliver rulings in halachah; an authority on Jewish law.

RASHA: an evil person.

RAV (pl. **RABBANIM**): a rabbi.

REBBE GELT: (Y.) lit., "money paid to a teacher" (the price of learning one of life's lessons).

REBBETZIN: (Y.) the wife of a rabbi.

ROSH YESHIVAH: the dean of a yeshivah.

SAVTA: grandmother.

SEDER (pl. **SEDARIM**): study session in a yeshivah.

SEFER TORAH: a Torah scroll.

SEUDAH: a meal.

SHADCHAN: a matchmaker.

SHADCHAN GELT: money paid to a matchmaker.

SHALOM BAYIS: lit., "peace [in the] home"; marital harmony.

SHEVA BERACHOS: the seven blessings recited at a wedding; any of the festive meals held in honor of the bride and groom during the week following the wedding, at which the seven blessings are recited.

SHIDDUCH (pl. **SHIDDUCHIM**): a marital match; a date.

SHIUR: a class.

SHIUR ALEPH: the first-year class in yeshivah.

SHIUR BEIS: the second-year class in yeshivah.

SHIUR GIMMEL: the third-year class in yeshivah.

SHKIYA: sunset.

SHLITA: an acronym for "May he live long."

SHTEIGED: (Y.) learn Torah assiduously.

SHTENDER (pl. **SHTENDERS**): (Y.) a wooden stand on which Jewish holy books are placed when they are studied.

SHTUSSIM: foolishness; nonsense.

SHVER: (Y.) father-in-law.

TEHILLIM: the Book of Psalms.

TEIRUTZ: resolution of a difficult question in Torah learning.

TESHUVAH: repentance.

TIKKUN: repair; fixing a spiritual blemish.

VORT: lit., "a word"; celebration of a couple's decision to become engaged.

YESHIVAH BACHUR: a yeshivah student.

YESHIVAH GEDOLAH: a Torah academy for post-high-school-age boys.

YESHIVAH KETANAH: a Torah academy for teenage boys.

YESHIVAH VELT: (Y.) yeshivah world.

Z"L: acronym for "*zichrono livracha*," may the memory of this person serve as a blessing, added when mentioning the name of a deceased individual worthy of respect.

ZIKUI HARABBIM: bringing merit to the masses.

ZMAN: lit., "time"; one of the three semesters in a yeshivah year.